What Every
Should Know

Basic Steps to Discipleship

LeRoy Eims

While this book is designed for the reader's personal use and profit, it is also intended for group study. A leader's guide is available from your local Christian bookstore or from the publisher.

VICTOR BOOKS

a division of SP Publications, Inc.
WHEATON, ILLINOIS 60187

Offices also in Fullerton, California • Whitby, Ontario, Canada • Amersham-on-the-Hill, Bucks, England

Sixth printing, 1980

Unless otherwise noted, Scripture quotations are from the King James Version. Other versions used are *The Living Bible* (LB), © by Tyndale House Publishers, Wheaton, Ill., used by permission; the *New Testament in Modern English* by J. B. Phillips (PH), © 1958, The Macmillan Company; and *The Amplified Bible* (AMP), © by Zondervan Publishing House, Grand Rapids, Mich.

Library of Congress Catalog Card Number: 75–44842
ISBN: 0-88207-727-9

© 1976 by SP Publications, Inc. World rights reserved
Printed in the United States of America

VICTOR BOOKS
A division of SP Publications, Inc.
P. O. Box 1825 ● Wheaton, Ill. 60187

Contents

To Waldron Scott
who taught me the life of discipleship

Preface

This book grew out of a memory. In the summer of 1954 I was in Ligonier, Pennsylvania speaking at a collegiate conference sponsored by the First Presbyterian Church of Pittsburgh. One night after the meeting, one of the dishwashing crew, a young man named John, came to me and began to ask questions about the things of the Lord. We had a warm, friendly discussion about his own personal relationship to Jesus Christ. That night he received Christ as Saviour and surrendered his life to the Lord.

Next morning I had an hour with him before he left for Boston to enroll as a freshman at MIT. I talked to him about his new faith in Christ, and promised to write him regularly.

That school year I wrote John scores of letters. Day after day I would think through what his particular needs as a new Christian might be, and would share the Scriptures and principles of discipleship with him. He began to grow and share his faith with others. During his school breaks he came to Pittsburgh and we had great times together in the Word. I prayed for him regularly. Today he is a minister of the Gospel.

This book contains the basic ideas that I shared with John in trying to help him, a growing Christian, become an established, fruitful disciple.

Growth is slow, but if we meet the conditions given in the Word of God it is sure. This book goes out with the prayer that you will find it a helpful guide on your pilgrimage of faith as you follow the Saviour as one of His disciples.

Prologue to Chapter 1

When you received the Lord Jesus Christ as your Saviour, you became a member of an important family—the family of God. In time, you will meet and have fellowship with thousands of your brothers and sisters in Christ. But at the start, you need an in-depth look at your new Father. As a child of God, you need to learn how to relate to your Father in heaven, and learn to love Him, trust Him, follow Him, and how to relax in the sure knowledge of your Father's love and care for you. What follows is intended to help you better understand this new relationship.

1

Getting to Know the Father

As a new Christian you are probably quite concerned about the kind of life you lived before you were saved. If you are, you need to understand what God thinks about it.

Your Father Knows You

I once knew a senior in college who had high hopes. On graduation he planned to work for a large and prestigious company at a high starting salary and marry the girl of his dreams, whom he had known for about two years. He was deeply in love with her, and admired her godly life. She was reared by God-fearing parents, and they had taught her well. She lived her faith.

One hang-up, however, kept the young man awake nights worrying about it. He was convinced that if the girl ever found out about some problems and incidents in his past, she would have nothing more to do with him. He lived in fear that she might discover the truth about him. I tried to assure him that if she was a Christian, she would certainly understand the grace of forgiveness and the fact that he was a completely new person in Christ.

"Nope," he said, "I'm afraid she would walk out of my life if she ever found out."

As I thought about this fear, it occurred to me that the love of God has a strength about it that is often lacking in human love. Think about it! God knows all about us—all about our thoughts, all about our past, all about our secret goals and ambitions—and still He loves us with a deep and everlasting love. We

7

need never try to hide anything from Him for fear of losing His love. He knows us and loves us anyway.

Consider this. Jesus said, "I am the Good Shepherd, and know My sheep, and am known of Mine" (John 10:14). He knows each of us personally as a father knows his child. As a child I used to go to our family reunions. Throughout the day adults would ask me, "And whose boy are you?" I would then learn that I was their third cousin or some distant relative.

Now God is not like those adults at our reunions—He has no third cousins. When you receive Christ into your life, you become a child of God. He knows you, and it is a fact that has eternal consequences.

Recently I was in Washington, D.C. and went by the Senate Building to see a friend. I walked into the office and asked his secretary if I could see the senator for a few minutes.

She replied, "Actually he is very busy right now. Could I help you?" She then asked if I had an appointment, or did I have some business with him, or was I from his state.

"No," I told her, "he's a friend of mine and I just dropped by to say hello."

When she began to explain how busy he was, I gave her my card and asked her to give it to him when she went in. In a few minutes he buzzed for her, so she took her shorthand pad and my card and went into his office. In a few minutes she came hurrying out of his office and with a big smile said, "You may go right in."

I did and the senator and I had a few minutes of wonderful fellowship together. It wasn't anything that I had done that made me welcome. It certainly wasn't my station in life or my bank account. There was nothing except the fact that he knew me and we had been friends for years. And because of that I was welcome in his office.

David understood this truth: "O Lord, Thou hast searched me, and known me. Thou knowest my downsitting and mine uprising, Thou understandest my thought afar off. Thou compassest my path and my lying down, and art acquainted with all my ways. For there is not a word in my tongue, but, lo, O Lord, Thou knowest it altogether" (Ps. 139:1-4). So it is with you.

When troubles come crashing in on you, you may wonder if God really understands and knows your situation. Does He really know all about you? Is His eye of love really on you? The answer, of course, is clear, and you can trust Him to see you through. The Bible says, "For now we see through a glass darkly, but then face to face; now I know in part, but then shall I know even as also I am known" (1 Cor. 13:12).

Your Father Loves You

No doubt, the little family was celebrating some special occasion and had decided to go to a fancy restaurant. You could tell they felt out of place, seated in this beautiful dining room, dressed in their Sunday best, with huge menus in their hands, trying to find something they could afford. A couple of fish dinners weren't too expensive, the chopped sirloin was priced fairly reasonably, and the chicken wasn't too bad. The little family read the menu, whispered among themselves, and got their signals straight. They knew what they could afford and were ready to order.

Their waiter was a tall, dark man with a European accent. He had read the situation and knew how uncomfortable they felt. So he did what he could to put them at ease. He smiled, made sure they felt welcome, and even suggested a couple of dishes that cost a bit less.

Soon everyone had placed his order, but one—the youngest boy. The waiter turned to him and said, "And what will you have, young man?"

"I would like chicken, please."

"A wonderful choice, sir. I know you'll like our chicken. It is delicious. And would you like french fries with it?"

"Yes, please, I'd like that."

The waiter smiled, bowed, thanked the family, and left.

The little boy sat there for a while, turned to his father, and said, "You know, Dad, that man thinks I'm people."

In the same way that the trained European waiter had not treated the boy as just another customer in a roomful of customers, but had treated him as an individual, so the Lord deals with us. Each of us is considered "people"—really His very own child. He knows that occasionally we are a bit ill at ease in His presence, and He takes special care to assure us of His love and care for us.

God's love is unconditional. I have watched people live their Christian lives under a cloud because of some past sin in their lives; and because of it, they thought that God could never really love them. It is true that fellowship with God can be broken and must be restored through confession, repentance, and the forsaking of a particular sin. But through it all God's love shines strong and sure. He never sees you as just somebody else in a roomful or a worldful of people. He knows all about your needs, hurts, desires, and problems. And He is concerned. His love is set on you and beams from His own heart to yours.

Trust Your Father's Love

The Living Bible beautifully explains a tremendous truth: "We need have no fear of Someone who loves us perfectly; His perfect love for us eliminates all dread of what He might do to us. If we are afraid, it is for fear of what He might do to us, and shows that we are not fully convinced that He really loves us" (1 John 4:18, LB).

Some years ago I was in San Francisco and saw a good example of this fact. A friend of mine introduced me to a girl named Maggie who played the guitar and sang folk songs at a popular downtown coffee shop. She had come with a friend of mine to a Christian rally where I had shared the Gospel. Maggie was quite interested in the message of Christ and asked if she could meet me after the rally. As we stood by the piano, I asked her about her relationship to God. She freely admitted: "Well, I've always had this terrible fear that He might send me off to Africa as a missionary." She explained to me that snakes and bugs and wild animals terrified her. She liked her neat apartment and clean sheets and air conditioning. She just didn't want to go to Africa.

As the conversation continued, I inquired about the place where she worked. Then I asked her if she went out with the men who hung around there.

"No," she said, "not very often."

"Why is that?" I asked.

"Frankly," she replied, smiling, "they are a bunch of creeps and I just don't feel secure when I'm with them."

"Tell me, Maggie, if you were to meet a guy who really loved you, whose only desire was to do what was best for you, who showered you with gifts and was willing to lay down his life rather than let any harm or danger come into your life, how would you feel around him? Secure or insecure? Do you think he could be trusted?"

Naturally she said yes. I smiled and told her that was what I was trying to arrange. I had been trying to introduce her to the Lord Jesus Christ. As we talked and as she thought about it, she saw that her fears were completely unfounded. She finally understood the love of God and that night became a Christian.

One of the most powerful things about the love of God is that it is unconditional. We don't earn it. Human love has a way of responding to a person who treats us well or does something that pleases us. Not so with God. And the greatest demonstration of that love was the cross. "But God commendeth His love toward us, in that, while we were yet sinners, Christ died for us" (Rom. 5:8). This is especially significant in light of the context: "For when we were yet without strength, in due time Christ died for the ungodly" (5:6).

At times the Lord shows us another side of His love. "And ye have forgotten the exhortation which speaketh unto you as unto children, 'My son, despise not thou the chastening of the Lord, nor faint when thou art rebuked of Him; for whom the Lord loveth He chasteneth, and scourgeth every son whom He receiveth'" (Heb. 12:5-6). When we go astray, the Lord finds it necessary at times to discipline us, to bring us back to the high position of His perfect will. He is faithful to His erring children. He always knows best and desires the best for us.

I've watched California farmers tend their crops. They close a gate in the irrigation ditch and cause the stream to change direction in order to water other plants downstream. In the same way, God is always upstream, discerning our needs, observing the turn of events in our lives, and arranging things for our good. Because He loves us, He is always ahead of us, anticipating and meeting our needs.

You Belong to God

In the Old Testament, the word *sanctify,* which means "to set apart," was often applied to places and things: the camp of Israel, the hill of Zion, the city of Jerusalem, the tabernacle, the temple. The Holy Land itself was a land set apart. The sanctuary or temple was set aside for God's use only. In the Holy of Holies, God made His presence known. In the light of that concept, reflect for a moment on what Paul said: "What? Know ye not that your body is the temple of the Holy Ghost which is in you, which ye have of God, and ye are not your own? For ye are bought with a price; therefore glorify God in your body, and in your spirit, which are God's" (1 Cor. 6:19-20).

We belong to God. In early European history a Gregorian was a person who was part of the household of Gregory. Therefore, a Christian by definition is a person who belongs to the household of Christ. We are joined to Him and are actually a part of Him.

Paul also said, "Know ye not that ye are the temple of God, and that the spirit of God dwelleth in you?" (1 Cor. 3:16) So our bodies are actually the temple of the Holy Spirit, set apart in the same way that the Old Testament temple was a place where God could place His name and He alone could use.

The terms *sanctified* or *separated* mean more than just having a family relationship with God, though they certainly mean that. But they have a deeper meaning. They mean participation in the very nature of God. "Whereby are given unto us exceeding great and precious promises, that by these ye might be partakers of the divine nature, having escaped the corruption that is in the world through lust" (2 Peter 1:4).

As God's child, one who belongs to Him, you can be assured of His constant watch care over you. The Lord is your Shepherd. The old hymn says: "Children of the heavenly Father / Safely in His bosom gather. / Nestling bird or star of heaven / Such a refuge ne'er was given."

You now belong to God. Where sin and Satan once held you in their grip, you have now been delivered into the loving hands of your heavenly Father, translated into the kingdom of His dear Son. Many rights and privileges now belong to you as a member of the royal household, as well as duties and responsibilities. Learn to live as a child of God.

Your Father Never Changes

The only constant in this world is change. Everything is changing: your shoes are wearing out, your hair is falling out, your toenails are growing, birds fly south, then north, your car is showing signs of wear, the house needs paint, the garden needs weeding, the grass needs cutting. Political leaders we thought we could trust yesterday prove false today. And, in some areas, change is accelerating. We just get used to some situation, find a way to live in it, and then it changes. All this can create emotional and psychological problems for us. If there were only a rock—a stable, firm, unchanging foundation somewhere—that a person could count on, build his life on, trust in knowing it would be the same yesterday, today, and forever. Well, thank God, there is!

Because He is the eternal, unchangeable God, His Word is the eternal and unchangeable Word. Jesus said we are to believe what the prophets have spoken (Luke 24:25). The Apostle Peter wrote, "Being born again, not of corruptible seed, but of incorruptible, by the Word of God, which liveth and abideth forever. For all flesh is as grass, and all the glory of man as the flower of grass. The grass withereth, and the flower thereof falleth away. But the Word of the Lord endureth for ever. And this is the Word by which the Gospel is preached unto you" (1 Peter 1:23-25). That means you can trust His power to the end.

His Word is reliable. That, of course, has been the focal point of the devil's attack, since the serpent whispered in the garden, "Yea, hath God said? Can you really trust His Word? Are you sure?"

When I was a child we used to visit my cousin Eva's farm out in the timber to pick gooseberries. Cousin Eva and Cousin Dean kept coon hounds, and every night, year after year, when the moon would come up, these hounds would bark at the moon. I never quite understood what they had against it that made them bark at it by the hour. Through it all, I observed something about the moon. In spite of being barked at night after night, year after year, it was absolutely unmoved. It just went sailing along in the sky untouched by the barking of the dogs.

Since the time of the Fall (Gen. 3), the Word of God has been under attack. Today men still write books telling us why the Bible can't be explained. Television talk shows interview scoffers who explain in scholarly tones why the Bible is unreliable. But I've observed something about the Word of God in all of this. It is absolutely unmoved. Year after year, century after century, it goes sailing along, providing words of comfort, peace, love, joy, and truth. In a world of change, when most things seem pretty shaky, the immutable truth of God is still there.

Your Father Is There
One summer I was talking to one of the most dejected men I have ever met. He sat slumped in his chair, his head resting in his

hands. The floods had come and had practically washed away his farm, ruined his crops, and demolished some of his buildings. He had lost nearly everything. He and his wife had worked long and hard, but now their dreams had been swept away in the flood. In trying to console him, I asked him, "Do you believe the Bible?"

He looked up, his eyes narrowed, and he nodded yes. I had an *Amplified New Testament* with me and asked him to turn to Hebrews and read: "Let your character *or* moral disposition be free from love of money—[including] greed, avarice, lust and craving for earthly possessions—and be satisfied with your present [circumstances and with what you have]; for He (God) Himself has said, 'I will not in any way fail you *nor* give you up *nor* leave you without support. [I will] not, [I will] not, [I will] not in any degree leave you helpless, *nor* forsake *nor* let [you] down, [relax My hold on you].—Assuredly not!" (Heb. 13:5, AMP)

He read it, reread it, then read it again. It was like a plate of food to a hungry man. When I saw him again about a year later, he said, "LeRoy, that verse of Scripture you shared with me has meant more this year than anything else in my life. It has been the thing that has kept me from giving up. Whenever things would look bleak, I'd quote it to myself and would be reminded that God was with me. And it's true. He was always there."

Times will come in your life when that fact will mean more to you than anything you have ever learned. It was true in a recent experience in my own life. I had left my wife in Copenhagen on her way to Germany while I flew across Russia to Seoul, Korea, to speak at a conference. We were to meet again in Moscow on our way to Helsinki, Finland.

When I arrived in Tokyo and called to confirm my flight to Korea, I was told a rather disquieting bit of news. I was on a waiting list on my return trip from Seoul to Tokyo, where I was to catch my plane to Moscow to meet Virginia. "How long a waiting list?" I asked.

"A very long list, Mr. Eims. Actually it's impossible for you to get on that plane."

Well, I *had* to be on that plane in order to get to Moscow. I couldn't leave my wife stranded in the middle of Russia without her knowing where I was. So I checked with the four other airlines that flew from Seoul to Tokyo. They were all full, each with a waiting list. What was I going to do? Well, I began to worry. That night in Tokyo I felt very weak, very frightened, and very lonesome. I tried to pray, but it didn't go very well. I tried to sleep, but sleep wouldn't come. I tossed and turned and stewed and fretted until the wee hours of the morning.

Then it happened. It came loud and clear. It was a verse of Scripture that I had memorized as a young Christian. "Have not I commanded thee? Be strong and of a good courage; be not afraid, neither be thou dismayed, for the Lord thy God is with thee whithersoever thou goest" (Josh. 1:9). It was both a rebuke and a comfort.

When I got on the plane for Seoul I knew God would get me back to Tokyo to catch the plane to meet my wife. And He did! In fact, because of a sudden government ban on traveling for its citizens, I came back from Seoul on a huge 747 with about eight people on it! I knew the Lord had not forsaken me. He was right there.

Your Father Will Meet Your Needs

A few years ago my wife and I opened up our home for a ministry to the cadets of the Air Force Academy in Colorado Springs. During their off hours, they would come over and play Ping-Pong, eat, talk, eat, play table hockey, eat, play chess, and eat. We thoroughly enjoyed these young men and were fixing up a room in the basement for them. The one thing we lacked was a big davenport for them to sit on. So one day my wife and I drove downtown to pick one out. It had to be rugged, with a cover that would clean easily when mustard or pop or hot chocolate spilled on it.

She found one that was the right size and the salesman assured us that it could take a beating. So I told the salesman we'd like to have it, but we didn't have any money and didn't have any prospects of getting any. But, I told him, "I've got this." I pulled out my New Testament and showed him, "But my God shall supply all your need according to His riches in glory by Christ Jesus" (Phil. 4:19). I asked him, "Do you believe that?"

He was a bit startled and said, "Well, I don't know; I guess so."

"So do I," I replied, "and I'm willing to trust that promise if you are." I explained to him that we were in Christian work and needed the davenport and we were sure God would supply. I said,

"If you'll ship out the davenport, I'll bring the money down as soon as God provides it."

He looked dumbfounded. He thought for a minute and, still with a puzzled look, called out to the back of the store, "Hey, Joe, get the truck. We're movin' this davenport." In less than a month, the Lord had supplied enough money to cover the cost, so I went down to the store and said, "Here's your money." I think he was a bit shocked by it all.

Abraham's life illustrates a powerful truth. God sent him into the land of Moriah with his only son, Isaac, for a strange encounter with faith. Abraham, the friend of God, was to be tested by the Lord to what most of us would consider the breaking point. He was to offer his son, whom he loved, on the altar of dedication to God. At the last minute, the Angel of the Lord intervened to spare Isaac. Later, "Abraham called the name of that place Jehovah-jireh, as it is said to this day, 'In the mount of the Lord it shall be seen'—————" (Gen. 22:14).

The name Jehovah-jireh is translated to mean "the Lord will see and provide." For a long time I wondered what the words *see* and *provide* had in common. Then I learned a beautiful and exciting truth. *Pro* means ahead or beforehand and *vide* is the Latin word from which we get "video," which means the ability to see. His provision is based on His prevision—His ability to see ahead —to know what my needs will be, and to provide for them. Jesus said, "Your Father knoweth what things you have need of, before you ask Him" (Matt. 6:8). God is ready, willing, and able to meet our needs.

Recently my friend Chuck Madden and I were leaving on a trip to Europe. The night before we were to board the plane for the East Coast, Chuck met a buddy of his for coffee in a restaurant near our house. During their time together, Chuck got a nosebleed and went to the men's room for some wet towels. When the nosebleed stopped, he left the restaurant. In the confusion he left his billfold in the booth. The wallet had all his credit cards and money for the trip. We were due to leave around 6:30 the next morning.

At 6 A.M. the phone rang. "Is Charles Douglas Madden there?"

"Yes."

"Tell him we have his billfold here at the restaurant." Chuck had planned for the trip for months. Would the money still be in the billfold? Why had the man called so early—and how did he know he was staying at my home? To this day we still don't know. Chuck's address is in California. I don't have answers to all these questions, but I do know that the money was all there—nothing had been touched. Chuck was thankful to God, who had seen to it that he had provision to make the trip.

Your Father Will Lead You

One of the fondest memories of my childhood was the 10-cent Saturday night movies. We would drive in from the farm with the eggs and cream. When these were tested, weighed, and sold, my mother would send me off to the movies to watch a cowboy show. Occasionally in the story on the screen, one of the townspeople would be taken to Boot Hill, and the people would gather while the parson opened the Book and read, "The Lord is my Shepherd; I shall not want." We didn't come to town on Sunday mornings, so I didn't know much about religion; but over the years on Saturday night I learned those words. Years later, when I became a Christian at the age of 24, those words took on an exciting meaning in my life.

Over and over again the Scriptures show that God guides His people. "For this God is our God for ever and ever; He will be our guide even unto death" (Ps. 48:14). But, how does God guide us? Often Christians who are seeking guidance from Him go about it in the wrong way, because their idea of the ways and means of God's guidance is distorted. In looking for supernatural signs, they overlook the guidance that is right at hand, and lay themselves open to all sorts of delusions and false experiences. Sometimes their mistake is to think of guidance as essentially inward prompting by the Holy Spirit apart from the written Word of God.

I recall a story I heard while I was in high school during World War II. It was a report concerning an American army unit in North Africa that had been captured by the Germans. The Americans were well-equipped with trucks, tanks, guns, food, water, and everything an army needs. But they had gotten lost in the desert. Somehow their communication with headquarters had been cut off and they were wandering around aimlessly. The Germans came along and gathered them up without a fight. Not knowing where they were or where they were going, the Americans fell easy prey to the enemy.

Don't make that tragic mistake. One of the prime means of guidance for your life is daily fellowship with God as you speak to Him in prayer and He communicates His will for you through His Word.

Recently I heard a story of a mountain climber who hired a guide to take him up the face of a sheer rock. They were hundreds of feet in the air when the guide turned back, hooked himself into the rock with his rope, leaned over, and cupped his hands for the climber to step on. When the man hesitated, the guide smiled and said, "Sir, I haven't lost a man yet."

So it is with the Lord. You can follow Him with absolute safety, certainty, and enjoyment. David said, "I have set the Lord always before me; because He is at my right hand, I shall not be moved" (Ps. 16:8).

Your Father Gives You Peace

During the time when every summer in America prompted a polio epidemic, my wife, Virginia, and I were living in Council Bluffs, Iowa. The newspaper gave daily reports of people who had been stricken, along with information on how to detect early symptoms of polio.

One Sunday afternoon Virginia told me she was experiencing some of the early signs of the disease. It was late afternoon, and we both felt that the best thing to do was to go to the evening service in our church and ask the people to pray. We walked to church and asked the pastor and congregation for their prayers. During the meeting special prayer was offered for her. On the way home we both noticed something strange—both of our hearts were at perfect peace, though Virginia still had the stiff neck and the fever. We felt we were experiencing the reality of God's promise: "Be careful for nothing; but in everything by prayer and supplication with thanksgiving let your request be made known unto God. And the peace of God, which passeth all understanding, shall keep your hearts and minds through Christ Jesus" (Phil. 4:6-7).

That happened to us when we were brand-new Christians. Three years later, while I was studying at the University of Washington and witnessing to a fellow student, he said, "Well, if I could find a religion that could give me peace of heart, peace of mind, and peace with God, I'd snap it up in a minute."

I told him, "Friend, you'll never find those things in a religion.

But there's a Person who can give it all." Peace of heart—"Peace I leave with you, My peace I give unto you; not as the world giveth, give I unto you. Let not your heart be troubled, neither let it be afraid" (John 14:27). Peace of mind—"Thou wilt keep him in perfect peace, whose mind is stayed on Thee, because he trusteth in Thee" (Isa. 26:3). Peace with God—"Therefore being justified by faith, we have peace with God through our Lord Jesus Christ" (Rom. 5:1).

I have a doctor friend in Oklahoma City. Some years ago Dave Stuart had a practice on the West Coast and made it his habit to ask each of his patients the question: "If you had an Aladdin's lamp and could have anything you wished for, what would it be?" The answers were surprising. In the many years he asked the same question, all but three of his patients wished for the same thing. One said she would ask for a better job for her husband; two said they would ask for money; and all the rest said they would like to have inner peace in their hearts. Dave, being a fine Christian and a student of the Scriptures, often used these opportunities to tell them his source of inner peace—God Himself.

Paul said, "Now the God of peace be with you all. Amen" (Rom. 15:33). God is the fountain of peace. Jesus Christ is the Prince of Peace. Peace is the stream that flows from the heart of God to the hearts of His children. To seek peace from any other source is vain. Our Father in heaven is the God of peace.

Virginia's polio scare reminded me of the story of two artists who were commissioned to paint a picture of peace. One showed a calm, pastoral scene. The other showed a small bird nesting in a niche by the seaside, with waves crashing and pounding all around but not reaching her nest. In the midst of the turmoil she had found a place of safety and security. Jesus said, "These things I have spoken unto you, that in Me ye might have peace. In the world ye shall have tribulation, but be of good cheer, I have overcome the world" (John 16:33).

The Apostle Paul frequently prayed, "Grace be unto you, and peace, from God our Father, and from the Lord Jesus Christ" (1 Cor. 1:3). Inner peace, the thing that Dave Stuart's patients were looking for, is a by-product of your experience of the grace of God.

Prologue to Chapter 2

Now that you've been introduced to your heavenly Father, you may wonder how this relationship is to continue or have meaning for you. Well, in one sense it will be patterned after life in any family— you begin to grow up and learn to talk. You hear your parents talk to you, and you learn to talk to them. But first, you hear them talk before you begin to do so. That's where the Word of God comes in.

The Bible is the means by which God speaks to you. It is vital to your spiritual growth and development. It is only as you open your Bible and begin to experience the blessings that come as God speaks to your heart through it that you will find spiritual strength and nourishment.

The older you grow as a Christian, the more you will come to appreciate and love the Scriptures; the more you dig into the Word, the more you will become a man of the Word. This chapter contains truths that have been helpful to me and to many Christians as they began their spiritual pilgrimages—just as you are doing now.

2

The Bible:

Your Father Speaks to You

The way health food stores, gyms, and health clubs are going up all over the place, one would think the whole world is on a physical fitness kick. Grown men in tennis shoes are running up and down the streets. Cereals are now fortified with about everything under the sun. That's great! All well and good. Like they say, "When you've got your health, you've got just about everything."

But how about keeping fit spiritually? The Bible says, "Take time and trouble to keep yourself spiritually fit. Bodily fitness has a certain value, but spiritual fitness is essential, both for this present life, and for the life to come" (1 Tim. 4:7, PH).

Keeping Spiritually Fit
The secret of spiritual fitness is pretty simple.

• First, proper diet. The spiritual food we need is the Word of God. "And now, brethren, I commend you to God, and to the Word of His grace, which is able to build you up, and to give you an inheritance among all them which are sanctified" (Acts 20:32).

• Second, spiritual breathing. I was talking to a physical-fitness instructor once, and he told me, "You're not breathing properly; you're only using part of your lungs. You need to breathe deeply." Prayer is the breath of the soul. You need to pray deeply—that is, deepen your prayer life. It is what the Bible calls effectual fervent prayer, or earnest prayer.

• The third thing is rest. I was feeling ill one day and went to my doctor, who said, "The only thing wrong with you is that you need some rest." In the spiritual realm, rest comes to the person who is living in obedience to the Lord. The person who knows what the Lord wants but is disobedient is ill at ease; he has no rest of spirit. God says, "O that thou hadst hearkened to My commandments! Then had thy peace been as a river" (Isa. 48:18).

• And last, of course, there is no fitness apart from exercise. This is especially true for the spiritual life. Spiritual exercise is witnessing. "Go ye," get up and go, and tell people about Jesus.

Just as food, proper breathing, sufficient rest, and exercise are necessary for physical fitness, so the Word of God, prayer, obedience, and witnessing are necessary to keep spiritually fit. And you need to keep these vital elements alive in your life while you maintain fellowship with others.

The Purpose of the Word

In our society Bibles are everywhere. They appear in our courtrooms; they show up in our motels, often in colors to match the rooms; they are found in our hospitals; they are distributed by chaplains to servicemen; they are all over the place.

The psalmist had some reasons for considering the Word important: "I will praise Thee with uprightness of heart, when I shall have learned Thy righteous judgments. I will keep Thy statutes; O forsake me not utterly" (Ps. 119:7-8). The Bible is given to help us learn how to live—not just to give us information. To learn the commands of God and not keep them is to learn in vain. The Bible's main purpose is not to teach us theology, but to teach us about life, to help us develop a life-style that reflects the person of Jesus Christ. So when we open the Scriptures we see Him on the path of life; we see Him handling difficult situations; we see Him responding in love to words of accusation and hate; we see Him calm in the midst of tumult; we see Him giving Himself to people who spit in His face. This is the life He wants to teach us to live— life with a capital L, life in high gear—life, and not just feeble existence.

Jesus said, "I am come that they might have life, and that they might have it more abundantly" (John 10:10). Abundant Life— revealed in Jesus Christ through the Scriptures. And Jesus said, "He that hath My commandments, and keepeth them, he it is that loveth Me; and he that loveth Me shall be loved of My Father, and I will love him, and will manifest Myself to him" (John 14:21).

So to keep the Word of God, to obey it is one way we show our love for the Lord, and to that person Jesus makes a wonderful promise: He will manifest Himself—reveal more and more of His wonderful love, mercy, grace, and peace. To be a creative, exciting person, whose life radiates blessing, challenge, and comfort, we must take on the characteristics of the most creative and exciting person who ever lived: the Lord Jesus Christ Himself.

So what is the purpose of the Bible? God has given it to us so that we might learn what it says and then go out and do it.

The Effect of the Word on Our Lives

Two things happen to us as we learn to feed on the Word of God. First, we begin to grow. Peter says, "As newborn babes, desire the sincere milk of the Word, that ye may grow thereby" (1 Peter 2:2).

I remember when our son Randy was born and we brought him home from the hospital. It was Thanksgiving Day, and our 27 dinner guests lined the front walk as my wife walked to the house. One of the young men played Brahms' "Lullaby" on the trumpet. The neighbors didn't know what to think. Randy was completely oblivious—he was asleep. For the next few months, that's about all he did: sleep and eat. He couldn't walk, talk, or do anything much except eat and sleep. But he was growing. Today he is 17, and I have a tough time when he and I arm wrestle. He beats me consistently.

Just as we grow physically, God has provided that we should grow spiritually by feeding on His Word. Jesus said, "Man shall not live by bread alone, but by every word that proceedeth out of the mouth of God" (Matt. 4:4). Job exclaimed, "Neither have I gone back from the commandment of His lips. I have esteemed the words of His mouth more than my necessary food" (Job 23:12). Paul challenged the Ephesian elders: "Now, brethren, I commend you to God, and to the Word of His grace, which is able to build you up" (Acts 20:32).

The second thing that happens when we get into the Word is that we begin to experience cleansing in our lives. Jesus said, "Now ye are clean through the word which I have spoken unto you" (John 15:3).

Many today are concerned about air pollution, water pollution, or noise pollution, but the greatest danger comes from pollution of the soul. The problem seems so great, for sin abounds on every hand. The newspapers and weekly magazines seem to be the chronicles of sin and corruption—in government, business, labor, the military—everywhere!

Jesus said, "For from within, out of the heart of men, proceed evil thoughts, adulteries, fornications, murders, thefts, covetousness, wickedness, deceit, lasciviousness, an evil eye, blasphemy, pride, foolishness; all these evil things come from within, and defile the man" (Mark 7:21-23). You see, if we are to clean up the world, if we are to see society changed for the better, it has to begin within the heart of man.

All the man-made solutions that are constantly appearing on the scene amount to nothing, and many of them do more harm than good. The answer to soul pollution is found only in the Bible, because the problem is within man, a spiritual problem that can only be dealt with by the Spirit of God: "Wherewithal shall a young man cleanse his way? By taking heed thereto according to Thy Word" (Ps. 119:9).

Recently I was speaking to a group of college students and I asked them if any of them had problems with their thought-lives. They all acknowledged that they did. When I asked them what they did to get victory over their evil thoughts, they didn't have satisfactory answers.

We can do one of two things; one works, and the other doesn't. One is to try to suppress these thoughts, and this doesn't work. It's like having a balloon in a bathtub. You push it down and it pops right back up. Suppressing doesn't work. The thing that does work is substitution: replace the evil thought with the Word of God. Jesus prayed for His disciples, "Sanctify them through Thy Word; Thy Word is truth" (John 17:17). Paul said, "That He might sanctify and cleanse it [the Church] with the washing of water by the Word" (Eph. 5:26). The psalmist wrote, concerning the same problem, "Wherewithal shall a young man cleanse his way? By taking heed thereto according to Thy Word . . . Thy Word have I hid in mine heart, that I might not sin against Thee" (Ps. 119:9, 11).

That is why the Word of God must be read carefully and prayerfully. We must give the Holy Spirit an opportunity to speak to us and to point out our sins and shortcomings. Then we should confess our sins and receive His cleansing. This is God's answer to the problem of pollution of the soul.

One night our cat got in a fight with a skunk, and the cat lost. The solution to the problem of his new smell was in washing the cat in soapy water and tomato juice. After generous applications of each, his presence finally became bearable. We had a specific remedy for a specific problem. So it is with our lives. Generous amounts of time spent with the Lord as He speaks to us through His Word is a must. Man-made solutions fail. God has given us His Word which is the cleansing agent the Holy Spirit uses for our sins (Titus 3:5).

The Delight of Our Lives

Be honest with yourself, and take a good look at how much time you spend with magazines, newspapers, and television in comparison with the time you spend reading your Bible. Many people have had their perspective completely changed as they have been confronted by the 119th psalm.

Start with this: "I will delight myself in Thy statutes; I will not forget Thy Word" (v. 16). Again the writer says, "O how love I Thy law! It is my meditation all the day" (v. 97). Later he states: "Thy testimonies are wonderful; therefore doth my soul keep them" (v. 129). And again: "Thy Word is very pure; therefore Thy servant loveth it" (v. 140). Now, isn't that something? Here was a man who had everything: power, prestige, wealth, popularity; but the thing in which he found his delight was the Word of God. Notice his deep feelings: "My soul breaketh for the longing that it hath unto Thy judgments at all times" (v. 20). Why did the Word of God mean so much to him? He says, "My soul cleaveth unto the dust; quicken Thou me according to Thy Word" (v. 25). God infused new life into him through the Word when he was feeling low.

All of us have times when we are blue and when our spirits droop, when gloom and discouragement settle over us. That is when we need the strong hand of God to lift us up. David describes it to us: "I waited patiently for the Lord, and He inclined unto me, and heard my cry. He brought me up also out of an horrible pit, out of the miry clay, and set my feet upon a rock, and established my goings. And He hath put a new song in my mouth, even praise unto our God. Many shall see it, and fear, and shall trust in the Lord" (Ps. 40:1-3). God revived him and infused him with new power.

Ask the Lord to make His Word sweet to your taste that you might find delight in His Word. Review again how the Lord used His Word in the life of the psalmist. Read the 119th psalm and jot down God's promises to the one who will give attendance to His Word.

A Daily Quiet Time

People who have been used of God are those who have met with God on a daily basis. They have so ordered their lives that they have found time to pray and read the Word of God. Quite often they do this in the early morning before work presses in, before the phone rings, and before the demands of the day are upon them. Most of us live busy lives. Few Christians feel they have all the time they need. Our families, our homes, our churches, our businesses, our community activities—all keep us hopping. But we need to get our priorities straight.

You will save a lot of time in morning prayers and Bible reading if you get yourself organized the night before. Take whatever you are going to use to the place where you plan to meet God: your Bible, devotional booklet, reading glasses, prayer lists. Have in mind the Scriptures you will read; have a plan. Have your clothes ready and laid out. When the alarm goes off, get up. And here's a tip: If you wind the alarm only half a turn, you will not wake the rest of the household. Wash your face with cold water. Take some deep breaths at the open window. Wake up!

When you get to the place of meeting, start by reading the Bible. This helps to get your mind on the Lord. When you begin your prayertime, if your mind starts to wander, pray aloud. If things come to mind that you need to do during the day, jot them down on a handy piece of paper. If you feel yourself getting drowsy, walk around the room while you pray. After a few weeks, if it seems you are getting in a rut, vary what you do. Pray over an open Bible, verse by verse. Pray over a map of the world, asking for God's blessing on His work in the remote corners of the mission fields of the world.

Scripture Memory—the Word in the Heart

I think two of the master strokes of the devil have been to convince people he doesn't exist, and to get Christians to believe that Scripture memory is only for children. He remembers the humility of defeat when Jesus Christ, who was tempted in all points like as we are, met him with the Word of God (Heb. 4:15). The prophets of the Old Testament and the apostles of the New both give stirring admonitions as to the value of having the Word of God in our hearts. Moses said, "These words . . . shall be in thine heart" (Deut. 6:6). Paul wrote, "Let the Word of Christ dwell in you richly in all wisdom" (Col. 3:16).

The only safe way to move through life is to have the Word of God with us always—in our hearts. Then when the allurements of sin come our way, we are better prepared for them, and can make our decisions based on the truth of God's Word.

Scripture memory pays great dividends, for it can be done in our spare moments. Redeem the time by spending a few minutes memorizing the Word of God. The great men and women of God of the past have demonstrated the worth of this practice.

A study of the lives of the prophets and apostles will make it apparent that they were men filled with God's Word. Jesus Himself is our prime example. Scripture memory is profitable for all of us, young and old alike.

Let me share with you some things I've learned about memorizing Scripture. You may think you are one of those who "just can't memorize." Let me ask you what comes to mind when I say, "Twinkle, twinkle, little _____"? Or, "Baa, baa, black _____"? Why do you think of *star* and *sheep?* Because you memorized these lines, and you remember them to this day. Now you didn't just hurriedly try to memorize the words, you overlearned them. Time and time again your mother or grandmother repeated the lines to you, reinforcing those words into your mind through repetition. You learned these nursery rhymes and you still remember them. So, we conclude that you *can* memorize. The secret of successful memorization is to review, review, review.

We also touched on another important principle. That is the principle of association. You associated "twinkle" with "star." Your mind tells you they go together. The reason so many people say, "I can't remember the reference," is that they have never taken the time to associate the reference with the verse. For instance, if you were to repeat 10 times, "John 3:16, 'For God so loved the world,' " guess what you'd associate with "For God so loved the world"? It's just like "twinkle, twinkle, little star"—association.

So hook the reference through repetition to the first few words of the verse. I can hear someone say, "But that's so tedious and mechanical." Believe me, everything is tedious and mechanical at first. Remember when you tried to learn to tie your shoe? play the piano? drive the car? As you continue the process of repetition, the material becomes part of your memory just like other things you have learned that way.

The blessings of having the Word of God in the heart are many. These are a few.

• It will give victory over sin. "Wherewithal shall a young man cleanse his way? By taking heed thereto according to Thy Word. . . . Thy Word have I hid in mine heart, that I might not sin against Thee" (Ps. 119:9, 11).

• It will bring joy to your soul. "These things have I spoken unto you, that My joy might remain in you, and that your joy might be full" (John 15:11).

• It will help you become a more effective witness for Christ as you authoritatively share what the Bible says.

If you have not yet enrolled in the Topical Memory System, I encourage you to do so. It will provide a balanced diet of Scripture intake that will bless your soul. The course will teach you the principles of memory that you can master and fill your heart with the Word of God. (It can be purchased in your local Christian bookstore, or ordered from The Navigators, P. O. Box 1659, Colorado Springs, Colo. 80901.)

Claiming God's Promises

When God promises to do something He means it. The Bible says, "God is not a man, that He should lie; neither the son of man, that He should repent; hath He said, and shall He not do it? Or hath He spoken, and shall He not make it good?" (Num. 23:19) Paul speaks of our God who cannot lie (Titus 1:2). Jesus said, "Thy Word is truth" (John 17:17).

The Bible also tells us that God has all the resources of the universe at His disposal: "Behold, I am the Lord, the God of all flesh; is there anything too hard for Me?" (Jer. 32:27) If God's promises are all true, and we know from His Word that He has the power and resources to fulfill them, then we should have expectant hearts, and take God at His Word.

There are a couple of keys to learning how to claim the promises of God. One is knowledge. The other is faith. We must know what God promises, and we must believe. Nehemiah is a vivid example of this. One day he heard of the terrible plight of his countrymen and his heart was burdened for them. He "sat down and wept, and mourned certain days, and fasted, and prayed before the God of heaven" (Neh. 1:4). He acknowledged to God that the situation the people were in was one of their own making. "We have dealt very corruptly against Thee, and have not kept the commandments, nor the statutes, nor the judgments, which Thou commandest Thy servant Moses" (1:7). Then he does an amazing thing. He asks God, who knows all and is eternal wisdom, to remember His own Word.

In effect, he takes the Bible, opens it to the Book of Leviticus and says, "God, do You remember writing this? Do you remember Your promise?" He said to the Lord: "Remember, I beseech Thee, the word that Thou commandest Thy servant Moses, saying, 'If ye transgress, I will scatter you abroad among the nations. But if ye turn unto Me, and keep My commandments, and do them; though there were of you cast out unto the uttermost part of heaven, yet will I gather them from thence, and will bring them unto the place that I have chosen to set my name there' " (1:8-9).

Imagine! Reminding God of His own Word! Then, on the basis of that promise he says to the Lord, "We qualify!" "Now these are Thy servants and Thy people, whom Thou hast redeemed by Thy great power, and by Thy strong hand" (1:10). Here is a man who saw a desperate situation, who claimed a promise of God, who launched out in faith on that promise, and God answered and fulfilled His Word. That, in essence, is *what it means* to claim the promises of God and *how to do it*.

I recall when God did something like that for me, only on a much smaller scale. I was attending the University of Washington, and winter was coming on. I was living on the G.I. Bill and barely making ends meet. Though the winters don't get bitter cold up there, it is chilly enough to require a jacket. But I didn't have one. I was a new Christian at the time, and had noted with great interest this verse: "My God shall supply all your need according to His riches in glory by Christ Jesus" (Phil. 4:19). I wasn't quite sure about it, but it seemed to say that since I was a child of God and had a legitimate need, I should be able to ask God to make that verse personal to me. So I prayed, reminded God of that verse, and asked Him for a jacket.

Time passed and the cold weather grew nearer, yet I saw no evidence of a jacket anywhere. But I hung on to that verse. One weekend I was in Tacoma with a doctor friend, who asked at the end of our day together, "Could you use a jacket? I've got this suede jacket that I never wear. Could you use it?"

Before I could answer he asked again, "And by the way, do you have a watch?"

As a matter of fact, I didn't have a watch and it was sort of a nuisance. Sometimes I was late for class or appointments, so I said, "Yes, I could use the jacket, and no, I don't have a watch."

I had other problems; for instance, my shoes had holes and there was lots of rain. The day after I was given the jacket and a watch a man gave me a pair of shoes. God had supplied my needs over and abundantly, not just barely, but according to His riches in glory.

Small things, you say? Sure they were. But they convinced me of the truth of God's Word, that God was able to keep His promises. And it set me on a course that has proven the faithfulness of God again and again. "Now unto Him that is able to do exceeding abundantly above all that we ask or think, according to the power that worketh in us" (Eph. 3:20).

Studying God's Word

Another attack of the devil is subtle and devastating. Unless it is exposed, your spiritual growth will be greatly hindered. The evil one has convinced thousands of Christians that Bible study is for the pastor and missionary, but is of no use for the ordinary Christian. Let's recognize it for what it is, a lie from the father of lies.

The simple truth is that God has given His Word to us so that we might enjoy its spiritual riches and receive blessings for our souls as we dig into it on our own. Bible study is for everyone. Let me share a few things that may help you study the Bible for yourself.

First, set aside some specific time during the week. Plan your schedule just as you would plan your mealtimes or your daily quiet time. Plan it into your schedule as you would an appointment with the doctor, an important client, or a golf game.

Second, study the Bible itself. There are many good books on the market, but none of them can take the place of the Bible. God wants to speak to you on a heart-to-heart basis—from His heart to yours. Reading what God has said to others is interesting, and reading books that record insights from God can be profitable. But the important thing is that your Father in heaven wants to speak to you, and to bless your soul directly from His Word.

Third, record your findings. Keep a spiritual journal of the things you receive from God. The advantages of jotting things down are that thoughts come clearer to you as you put them on paper; vague impressions or unclear thoughts untangle themselves as you write them down. And when they are on paper, you don't have to worry about forgetting them.

Fourth, make your study application-oriented. Look for those things which will make you a better person, things you can apply to *how* you live. Some of the most cantankerous and cranky people I know are loaded with Bible *facts*. They can name the minor prophets, the years of the falls of Jerusalem and Babylon, the width of the wall of Jericho, and so on. But the point of the Bible is to help you *do* something about your bad attitude or thought-life or sharp tongue. The prophet said, "Let us search and try our ways, and turn again to the Lord" (Lam. 3:40). David said, "I thought on my ways, and turned my feet unto Thy testimonies" (Ps. 119:59).

One of the things I needed as a young Christian was a definite plan to help me get started. A simple plan of Bible study that I heartily recommend is "Design for Discipleship," published by The Navigators. (You can obtain it from your local Christian bookstore, or write to the publisher at P. O. Box 1659, Colorado Springs, Colo. 80901.) It will help start you on the great adventure of digging into the Bible, the greatest of all books.

Reading the Word of God Devotionally

A little time spent reading the Bible every morning can surely give you a fresh outlook on life. It can lift your spirit, infuse you with hope, and draw your mind to eternal things. Most of all, it gets you in touch with God. And that's what's important!

Don't be in a hurry when you read. Just settle back and let the Spirit of God speak to your heart. "For the Word of God is quick, and powerful, and sharper than any two-edged sword, piercing even to the dividing asunder of soul and spirit, and of the joints and marrow, and is a discerner of the thoughts and intents of the heart" (Heb. 4:12). If the Holy Spirit speaks to you about some hidden sin or failure, stop what you are doing, and talk it over with the Lord. Confess your sin and expect His cleansing. Remember: "If we confess our sins, He is faithful and just to forgive us our sins, and to cleanse us from all unrighteousness" (1 John 1:9).

Take special note when you read of God's dealing with His people. Very likely if God was displeased with something back when the Scriptures were written, He feels the same way about it today. God's standards of holiness and righteousness do not change. So, read in a meditative frame of mind, ever alert to the Holy Spirit who might want to correct something in your life and put you back on the right track. Note especially what Paul said when you read the Old Testament: "Now all these things happened unto them for ensamples; and they are written for our admonition, upon whom the ends of the world are come" (1 Cor. 10:11).

Meditating on the Word
Meditation today is a lost art. We are people on the go, active, busy, and in a hurry. So the idea of taking out a portion of a day to sit and do nothing but reflect might be considered a waste of time.

However, God in His Word commands us to slow down, sit down, and think upon His Word. "Meditate upon these things; give thyself wholly to them, that thy profiting may appear to all" (1 Tim. 4:15).

The word *meditate* carries with it the idea of depth. It calls to mind the deep bass keys on the piano keyboard, a deep tone rather than a high and light one. To meditate takes discipline and time. We are more prone to "go over" lightly rather than take the time to search out the depth of meaning. We would rather pick a few loose nuggets on the hillside than dig for the treasure hidden in the earth.

There is a good reason why we should meditate on God's Word. God has made some staggering promises to the man or woman who will give serious thought and attention to His Word. Consider just two of them. "This book of the law shall not depart out of thy mouth, but thou shalt meditate therein day and night, that thou mayest observe to do according to all that is written therein; for then thou shalt make thy way prosperous, and then thou shalt have good success" (Josh. 1:8). God promises success to the person who will meditate on His Word.

Joshua was not an idle man. He was up to his neck in the serious business of providing leadership for thousands of people. This word from God came to him at a time when he was busier than he had ever been in his life, and was carrying greater responsibility than he had ever imagined in his wildest dreams. In the midst of his battle campaigns and all the problems of leadership, the Word of God was to be central in his thinking.

Another promise, in the Psalms, is lost to many people because it is so familiar. Children memorize it in Sunday School and Vacation Bible School, and pastors quote it from the pulpit. The words are charming and melodic, but they are also absolutely true. God meant it when He said, "Blessed is the man that walketh not in the counsel of the ungodly, nor standeth in the way of sinners, nor sitteth in the seat of the scornful. But his delight is in the law of the Lord, and in His law doth he meditate day and night. And he shall be like a tree planted by the rivers of water, that bringeth forth his fruit in his season; his leaf also shall not wither; and whatsoever he doeth shall prosper" (Ps. 1:1-3).

Let those words jar you: "Whatsoever he doeth shall prosper." Can that really be true? There's only one way to find out. Try it!

OK, you say, how do I go about meditating on God's Word? Let me tell you right off that it is not easy. It requires two things that most of us don't usually have: time and discipline. You make time for what you consider important. You eat, sleep, and take showers. Meditation will require your planning an appointment with God, a time when God can communicate to you through His open Word. That takes discipline.

To help you get started, let me suggest a simple plan. Tomorrow, set aside a period of time for Bible reading. Start with the Psalms. Read one or two with a prayer that the Holy Spirit will open His Word to you. As you read, pause when some thought or phrase stands out. Think of its meaning to your own situation. Turn it over and over in your mind. Let it sink in. Consider what it might mean to you and your family situation, your job, your relationship to God. Don't hurry the process. Say it out loud. Think. After you have mentally chewed on it for a while, pray over it. Ask the Lord to work it into your spiritual bloodstream by His Spirit.

Meditation is tough, but rewarding. If you can make it over the first few hurdles, you will establish a life-style on the highest plane. You will find yourself truly walking with God.

The Wonder of the Word

While you are at Disneyland, you visit many lands: Frontierland, Tomorrowland, Fantasyland, Adventureland. But you hunt there in vain for Wonderland. You won't really find that till you get back home and open the pages of that old book with the name Holy Bible. The psalmist says, "Open thou mine eyes, that I may behold wondrous things out of Thy law" (Ps. 119:18). Jeremiah wrote, "The Lord will deal with us according to all His wondrous works" (Jer. 21:2)

The Bible tells you of God's dealing with His people down through the ages. You'll find Him leading Abraham, His friend, through many a dangerous and treacherous situation. You'll find Him speaking to David, encouraging him, and giving him many great and precious promises. And as you look at these events, you will be reminded that all these things happened to God's ancient people so that they might be examples—for your sake. Paul says, "Whatsoever things were written aforetime were written for our learning, that we through patience and comfort of the Scriptures might have hope" (Rom. 15:4).

God uses His Word in our lives in a variety of ways. We are born into God's family by the Word (1 Peter 1:23); we grow by the Word (1 Peter 2:2); we are cleansed by the Word (John 15:3); we are sanctified by the Word (John 17:17); we are protected by the Word (Eph. 6:17); we are built up by the Word (Acts 20:32); we are guided by the Word (Ps. 119:105); we are converted by the Word (Ps. 19:7); we are satisfied by the Word (Ps. 119:103).

For the Bible to be all this, and more, it must be of divine origin. The Bible says, "All Scripture is given by inspiration of God" (2 Tim. 3:16). The meaning of the word translated *inspiration* is "God-breathed." This does not mean that after the Book was written God somehow breathed His divine stamp of approval into it. What it actually means is "breathed out"—the Scriptures are God's very breath.

In spite of having been written by more than 35 authors over a period of 1500 years, it is logically consistent and displays a remarkable unity. For this to have happened without a superintending or overseeing hand would have to be regarded as a most remarkable accident. Historical and archaeological confirmation of the truth of the Bible is of great embarrassment to those who would try to disprove it. Every spade of dirt and sand that has un-covered material relevant to the Bible has confirmed the reliability of the Scriptures.

The Bible is God's Word to you. Believe it, claim its promises, and obey its commands. "The Word is very nigh unto thee, in thy mouth, and in thy heart, that thou mayest do it" (Deut. 30:14).

Prologue to Chapter 3

God speaks to you through His Word. Your part of the conversation is prayer. You will find as you grow up in the Lord that prayer is more than just a comforting psychological experience. It is conversation and communion with God.

Your daily schedule is full. You have a job to think about. You are a working person, or a busy housewife with children to think about. You are a student with assignments to do and your courses are tough. You consider most of your activities important or you wouldn't do them. But prayer is more than just important—it is a matter of life or death as far as spiritual growth is concerned.

As you don't really get to know your Father till you let Him speak to you through His Word, so the father-child relationship cannot deepen unless you converse with Him, and share your problems, your burdens, your worries, and your joys. Children often complain that their parents never listen to them. Well, you'll never have that problem with your Father—He wants you to talk to Him.

3
Prayer: You Talk to Your Father

If your growth and development depend on your relationship to God, then certainly your effectiveness as a testimony for Him depends on your prayer life. As the Word of God is the source of power, prayer could be considered the channel for power.

Many Christians would like to be effective in their witness, but are not sure how to go about it. Jesus said of His disciples: "Ye are the light of the world" (Matt. 5:14). It is obvious from the daily news and television that our sin-darkened world needs the kind of clear and shiny light that Jesus desired of His followers.

A Life That Shines

One summer my son Randy and I spent a month together in a training program at a church in Honolulu. We were doing a Bible study together one night and came across the question, "How should we appear in the world?" The answer was to be found in Philippians 2:15: "That ye may be blameless and harmless, the sons of God, without rebuke, in the midst of a crooked and perverse nation, among whom ye shine as lights in the world." Randy looked at that verse for a while and then wrote down, "Be shiny."

When I saw what he had written, I thought, *Man, that's right! Be shiny! Especially when the world around us is described as crooked and perverse.* But we have a problem. We have no light within ourselves that will naturally shine in a darkened world. The only way we can shine is to reflect the light of Jesus Christ— the Light of the world.

Shortly after I got out of the Marine Corps following World War II, I worked as a telegrapher and depot agent for the Chicago Great Western Railroad. One of the jobs of the depot agent in those days was to receive train orders over the telegraph wire and pass them along to the trains as they went by the station. We would hold up a long forked stick to which the orders were tied, and the engineer in front and the conductor could put an arm through the fork in the stick and catch the message strung between the prongs.

It was a good method and worked well, except at night. At night the engineer might miss the order because he couldn't see the fork in the stick. He would then have to stop the train, back up to the station, and get the message attached to the stick. Of course, he would be furious, because I hadn't held the stick in the right place.

After a while someone came up with the bright idea of painting the stick with luminous paint so it would shine in the dark. It was a great idea and helped tremendously. All I had to do was hold the forked end of the stick up to the light for a few seconds, go outside, and it would shine in the dark. Occasionally, though, I would get busy with something else, hear the train coming, attach the signals for the engineer, grab the stick, and forget to hold it up to the light. Naturally, it didn't shine and sometimes he would miss it.

Some of my days have gone that way on occasion also. I get up in the morning, get busy, the phone begins to ring, I grab a quick breakfast, and off to a day full of activity. If I keep that sort of thing up for very long, I don't do much shining. What I need to do is to make certain that I have a regular time with the Lord just to bask in His presence, to spend time in His Word, and to let Him speak to my heart, and then to spend some time in prayer and share my heart with Him. I need this time because I have no light of my own. I only shine when I, like the forked stick, am placed near the source of light. I need to reflect the light of Jesus Christ, and I can't do that unless I am frequently in His presence.

The Joy of Daily Time Alone with God
Mark records this significant fact about Jesus: "And in the morning, rising up a great while before day, He went out, and

departed into a solitary place, and there prayed" (Mark 1:35). The Old Testament tells us that "Abraham got up early in the morning to the place where he stood before the Lord" (Gen. 19:27).

It is important to remember that men who have been mightily used of God through the ages have maintained this time alone with Him. David said, "My voice shalt Thou hear in the morning, O Lord; in the morning will I direct my prayer unto Thee, and will look up" (Ps. 5:3). If the outlook is grim, look to God in daily prayer.

Daniel also is a challenge to our prayer lives. The king had signed a decree saying that if anyone prayed to any God or man other than the king, he would be thrown to the lions. "Now when Daniel knew that the writing was signed, . . . he kneeled upon his knees . . . and prayed and gave thanks before his God" (Daniel 6:10). Daniel was a man who would rather die than miss his time alone with the Lord.

An important lesson to learn is to get ready the night before for the time alone with God in the morning. Hours that could be spent in productive sleep are often wasted in unproductive chatter or staring at the television. Note what the Lord told Moses: "Be ready in the morning, and come up in the morning unto Mount Sinai, and present thyself there to Me" (Ex. 34:2).

You might ask, "Why should we spend time alone with God?" Paul answers the question: "God is faithful, by whom ye were called unto the fellowship of His Son Jesus Christ our Lord" (1 Cor. 1:9). God made us for fellowship with Himself! He walked with Adam in the cool of the day in a warm and loving fellowship in antiquity. And Jesus Christ died in order that we might have intimate, personal fellowship with God.

We see how eager God is for fellowship with us by reflecting on what happened the moment our Lord died on the cross. The Bible says, "Jesus, when He had cried again with a loud voice, yielded up the ghost. And, behold, the veil of the temple was rent in twain from the top to the bottom" (Matt. 27:50-51). At that instant God made the way clear for us to enter into the Holy of Holies into His very presence—to enjoy intimate, personal fellowship with Him. Jesus Christ died to make that possible.

The spirit of God uses this daily fellowship to transform us more and more into the likeness of Jesus. The Bible says that

God wants us to be conformed to the image of His Son (Rom 8:29).

Many people have asked, "Just what do you *do* during this time?" Well, I've done a number of things, but by and large, I spend time in simple conversation with God. I read His word, through which God speaks to my heart, and then I pray and share my heart with God. It is important to remember that God really listens to us. He hears the cry of our hearts.

Conditions for Answered Prayer

Prayers are answered only on the *basis* of Christ's saving work on the cross, and not because of anything we can do. Yet, the Bible reveals that there are certain *conditions* that we must meet in order to pray effectively. Despite God's grace and the work of Christ, there are certain acts which God has chosen not to do for us except as we meet the conditions that He has laid down for us. God hears our prayers as we pray on His terms laid down in Scripture.

The first condition is to pray in Jesus' name. Jesus told His disciples, "Hitherto have ye asked nothing in My name; ask, and ye shall receive, that your joy may be full" (John 16:24). We can enter into the very presence of God by a new and living way, Jesus, who said, "I am the way" (John 14:6). Paul emphasized this truth by stating, "There is one God, and one mediator between God and men, the man Christ Jesus" (1 Tim. 2:5). If we want God to hear and answer our prayers, we must pray in Jesus' name.

Second, we are to pray in God's will. John says, "This is the confidence that we have in Him, that, if we ask anything according to His will, He heareth us; and if we know that He hear us, whatsoever we ask, we know that we have the petitions that we desired of Him" (1 John 5:14-15). Jesus prayed, "Not My will, but Thine, be done" (Luke 22:42), and this should be our attitude as well. God is our loving heavenly Father, and He knows what is best for us. My children have asked me for things that I knew would be wrong for them. Because I loved them, and wanted the best for them, I had to say no. God responds in the same way. He says, yes, no, or wait.

Third, prayer should be in accordance with God's power. The Lord spoke to Jeremiah and said, "Call unto Me, and I will answer thee, and show thee great and mighty things which thou knowest not" (Jer. 33:3). As a young Christian, I was challenged by Dawson Trotman, founder of The Navigators, when he asked, "Are you praying for continents or for toys?" We rarely give God a chance to demonstrate His power because of our small prayers.

Fourth, prayer should be specific. The great promise of Jesus Christ is: "Whatsoever ye shall ask in My name, that will I do, that the Father may be glorified in the Son. If ye shall ask anything in My name, I will do it" (John 14:13-14). Ask great things of God. Expect great things from God. Pray about everything. Note Paul's words; "Be careful for nothing, but in everything by prayer and supplication with thanksgiving let your requests be made known unto God. And the peace of God, which passeth all understanding, shall keep your hearts and minds through Christ Jesus" (Phil. 4:6-7).

Fifth, we must be persistent. The Bible says we ought always to pray and not lose heart. God hears the earnest, fervent prayer of the person who lays hold on God and cries out, "I will not let Thee go, except Thou bless me" (Gen. 32:26).

The Bible also tells of three hindrances to prayer. The first is unconfessed sin in the life of a Christian. "If I regard iniquity in my heart," the psalmist said, "the Lord will not hear me" (Ps. 66:18). John reminds us: "Whatsoever we ask, we receive of Him, because we keep His commandments, and do those things that are pleasing in His sight" (1 John 3:22). It is difficult to talk to God in prayer if we are out of fellowship with Him. Sin must be confessed and forsaken (see 1 John 1:9).

A second hindrance is unbelief. "All things, whatsoever ye shall ask in prayer, believing, ye shall receive" (Matt. 21:22). And James tells us: "Let him ask in faith, nothing wavering. For he that wavereth is like a wave of the sea driven with the wind and tossed. Let not that man think he shall receive anything of the Lord" (James 1:6-7). God delights to answer the prayer of faith.

A third hindrance to prayer is neglecting the Word of God. "He that turneth away his ear from hearing the law, even his prayer shall be abomination" (Prov. 28:9). And Jesus reminds His disciples, "If ye abide in Me, and My words abide in you, ye shall ask what ye will, and it will be done unto you" (John 15:7).

These principles, warnings, and directions for prayer are not meant to be obstacles to our prayer lives, but stepping-stones to power through prayer. God wants us to pray. He waits for us to pray. Thus the plea of the writer to the Hebrews: "Let us therefore come boldly unto the throne of grace, that we may obtain mercy, and find grace to help in time of need" (Heb. 4:16).

Christ Is Our Example

The Lord Jesus is the best example we will ever have of how to pray, as He is an example to us in all aspects of life. If we really want to learn to pray we should study how He spoke to His Father.

He prayed alone. "And in the morning, rising up a great while before day, He went out, and departed into a solitary place, and there prayed" (Mark 1:35). The Bible urges us to "pray without ceasing" (1 Thes. 5:17). On our knees, alone before God, our lives can have an effect around the world. Prayer changes things, prayer changes people, prayer changes the person who prays. There is merit in group praying, public prayers, even family devotions and prayers. But, nothing should take the place of our praying alone.

Second, Jesus prayed before major decisions. "It came to pass in those days, that He went out into a mountain to pray, and continued all night in prayer to God; and when it was day, He called unto Him His disciples, and of them He chose twelve whom He also named apostles" (Luke 6:12-13). Such a choice we would consider a major decision, and Jesus prayed all night before He made it. When we face things that are too much for us, and when we have decisions too hard for us, we know where we can turn for help. There is a need for regular times of prayer, but special decisions call for special times of prayer.

Third, He prayed in the midst of a busy schedule. "But so much the more went there a fame abroad of Him, and great multitudes came together to hear, and to be healed by Him of their infirmities. And He withdrew Himself into the wilderness, and prayed" (Luke 5:15-16). Jesus knew how to do the important, the priority thing, in the midst of secondary things that were pressing. Often being too busy is merely another excuse not to pray. Prayer works, but prayer *is* work. It's hard to pray. Our flesh resists entering the presence of a Holy God. But we must pray, and we must pray without ceasing.

Kinds of Prayer

The Bible teaches five different kinds of prayer. The first is *confession:* "If we confess our sins, He is faithful and just to forgive us our sins, and to cleanse us from all unrighteousness" (1 John 1:9). The word *confess* in the Greek is *homologeō,* combining *homoiōs,* "the same," with *legō,* "I speak." So to confess is to say the same thing about sin that God says. It is to have the same attitude toward sin that He has.

I served with the Marines in the South Pacific during World War II. One day I saw some large flat rocks on the beach of a tropical island. I turned one of them over and to my amazement saw hundreds of strange-looking, slimy, crawling things dart for another hiding place. They didn't want the light to shine on them; they enjoyed living in the dark. Confession is like turning over the rocks in our hearts and exposing our sins to the light of God, so that He may deal with them.

The Bible says, "He that covereth his sins shall not prosper, but whoso confesseth and forsaketh them shall have mercy" (Prov. 28:13).

The second kind of prayer is *praise.* God says, "Whoso offereth praise glorifieth Me" (Ps. 50:23). The prophet said, "O Lord, Thou art my God; I will exalt Thee; I will praise Thy name" (Isa. 25:1). There have been times in my life when the situation seemed so hopeless that I just couldn't pray. So I would stop and begin praising the Lord. I would praise Him for who He is, the creator of Heaven and earth; I would praise Him for His matchless power and amazing grace, for His love and mercy and goodness. Soon the cloud would life, my spirits would soar, and I would be on top again. When things get too tough even for prayer, try praise.

Humility is one of the crowning virtues of the Christian. It should be a natural fruit of praise. Its opposite, pride, is that sin which changed angels into devils. Satan, a powerful and glorious member of the heavenly host, one day was cast forth from the presence of God because pride had entered his heart and he had said, "I will be exalted." Pride, then, is a sin that bears bitter fruit.

Pride causes us to become insensitive of others. We think only about ourselves, not of others. It hinders our ministry because it detracts from the glory of God. "I am the Lord; that is My name;

and My glory will I not give to another, neither My praise to graven images" (Isa. 42:8). We find ourselves being resisted rather than blessed by the Lord. The Bible says, "God resisteth the proud, and giveth grace to the humble" (1 Peter 5:5).

If you and I reflect frequently on the nature of God, His power, righteousness, and love, and then think that in love He would stoop to die on a cross for our sins, this should cause us to exclaim: "Oh, God, who am I to be so blessed!" This should cause us to cast ourselves at His feet in thanksgiving and praise, in a spirit of true humility.

The desire of God's heart for us is to have us live before Him in beautiful fellowship, full of devotion and praise. A life of praise, then, is a life occupied with God Himself, not His gifts, not what He has done for us, but who He is as we stand in awe at the splendor of His person. "Whoso offereth praise glorifieth Me; and to him that ordereth his [conduct] aright will I show the salvation of God" (Ps. 50:23).

Thanksgiving is the third kind of prayer. The Bible says, "Offer unto God thanksgiving, and pay thy vows unto the Most High. And call upon Me in the day of trouble; I will deliver thee, and thou shalt glorify Me" (Ps. 50:14-15). Paul says "All things are for your sakes, that the abundant grace might through the thanksgiving of many redound to the glory of God" (2 Cor. 4:15). "In everything give thanks, for this is the will of God in Christ Jesus concerning you" (1 Thes. 5:18).

"Be careful for nothing, but in everything by prayer and supplication with thanksgiving let your requests be known unto God. And the peace of God which passeth all understanding, shall keep your hearts and minds through Christ Jesus" (Phil. 4:6-7). Thanksgiving as a consistent way of life is an exciting and rewarding life-style to fill our days here on earth. It's not easy, but it's the best.

Let's distinguish between thanksgiving and praise. Thanksgiving is necessary for the Christian. An unthankful heart is an abomination to the Lord. Do you remember the story of the 10 lepers who were healed by Jesus? "And one of them, when he saw that he was healed, turned back, and with a loud voice glorified God, and fell down on his face at His feet, giving Him thanks; and he was a Samaritan. And Jesus answering said, 'Were there not 10 cleansed? But where are the nine?'" (Luke 17:15-17) In

Paul's letter to the Romans, along with their worship of idols and uncleanness of life ungodly people are characterized as: "Neither were thankful" (Rom. 1:21). Thankfulness must be the life-style of the Christian.

Praise has to do with an overflow of our hearts in response to who God is; we extol His majesty, love, power, grace, long-suffering, kindness, and the splendor of His Person. The psalmist says, "I will praise Thee with uprightness of heart, when I shall have learned Thy righteous judgments" (Ps. 119:7). One of the chief values of living a life of praise is that it sets us into the life-style of the angels of God. They surround the throne of God and constantly praise, "Holy, Holy, Holy, Lord God Almighty" (Rev. 4:8). Praise, then, calls to mind the character and power of God. When we think on God's holiness and power, we are reminded of our own sinfulness and weakness. That should cast us completely on the Lord.

The next kind of prayer is *intercession*. We read of Paul's testimony to his friend: "Epaphras, who is one of you, a servant of Christ, saluteth you, always laboring fervently for you in prayers, that ye may stand perfect and complete in all the will of God" (Col. 4:12). Praying for others is a powerful means of living a life that has impact and significance.

If a person is hungry, give him food. If the person is thirsty, give him a glass of water. If the person is cold, invite him in by the stove or give him a coat. If he is unemployed, try to help him find work. If he has no place to live, help him find shelter. And so the list goes on. But the most meaningful help you can give a person is largely overlooked in this materialistic and secular age: Prayer—intercessory prayer.

People promise to do many things for others in need that do absolutely no good. I heard of a fellow who needed a job and was on his way to an interview. The man's friend heard about it and said, "I sure hope you get the job. I'll keep my fingers crossed." The man did get the job, came back to his friend, and said, "That's the best answer to crossed fingers I ever heard of!"

Unfortunately, there are those who put prayer in the same category. Just a nice little expression of concern, a way to tell a person you are involved and interested. But don't you believe it. Prayer is power, for behind believing prayer stand the immutable and unchangeable promises of God. The Prophet Samuel, who came to comfort the people of Israel, warned them not to turn to things which could not profit nor deliver, "For they are vain," he said. Then he made this powerful and dramatic statement: "Moreover as for me, God forbid that I should sin against the Lord in ceasing to pray for you" (1 Sam. 12:21, 23). Immediately after Samuel's warning, he assured them of his unceasing prayers. Prayer is profitable. Intercession can help.

I read of a missionary who was serving the Lord among people of a wild and dangerous tribe. The fiercest men of the tribe had determined to kill him, and came to his house one night to murder him. They were approaching the place when all at once they turned and ran. They had seen something that had gripped them with terror. Later, when these men were converted to Christ, they told the missionary about it. They had seen eight shining men with drawn swords standing guard around his home. Naturally, the missionary was surprised by the story, only to learn later that on the very night of the attack eight men in America had gathered to pray for the missionary's safety and protection. Think of that in light of the psalmist's declaration: "He orders His angels to protect you wherever you go" (Ps. 91:11, LB).

The New Testament speaks often of prayer for others, and some of the most helpful passages are the prayers of the Apostle Paul. In them we catch a glimpse of his great heart and his concern for others. "For this cause we also, since the day we heard it, do not cease to pray for you, and to desire that ye might be filled with the knowledge of His will in all wisdom and spiritual understanding; that ye might walk worthy of the Lord unto all pleasing, being fruitful in every good work, and increasing in the knowledge of God" (Col. 1:9-10). The entire prayer, along with those recorded in his other writings, provide us with a great source of inspiration and instruction in praying for others.

The last kind of prayer is *petition,* praying things for yourself. A well-known example is in the Lord's Prayer: "Give us this day our daily bread" (Matt. 6:11).

Like many young Christians, I really had a desire to follow the Lord. The preacher had spoken on the subject of prayer and given the challenge for us to become men and women who learned to pour out our hearts to God. I read books on the subject and was inspired by the lives of men such as Martin Luther and George Mueller, who spent hours every day on their knees. So, armed with a headful of information and a heartful of good intentions. I went to my knees. I prayed about everything I could think of with all the fervency I could muster, and arose from my place of prayer feeling that God must have taken note of a new prayer giant in the earth. I glanced at my watch and almost collapsed from surprise. About three minutes had elapsed.

The Bible gives us direction as to what we should pray for ourselves. The question of praying for ourselves arose when I was a young college worker in a program of evangelism and follow-up at a large Eastern university. We had seen a number of young men come to Christ and were in the process of helping them become established in a meaningful prayer life when the chaplain asked me to drop by his office. The next morning I went in to see him and after a brief chat he came to the point.

"Young man," he said, "I understand you are teaching students at the university that they should pray and ask God for things for themselves." Well, though that hadn't been the primary thrust of our study together, I had to admit that it was true. He looked at me with his sternest professional glare and said, "I want that stopped. I believe we should never pray for ourselves but only for others. To pray for yourself is a selfish and self-centered attitude in prayer."

I thought to myself that he certainly had a good emphasis and admired him for his sacrificial spirit and concern for others, but there was just one thing wrong. It was not scriptural. So I smiled and said, "Chaplain, would you mind if we read a verse of Scripture together?"

"Certainly not," he replied.

So I opened my Bible and read Matthew 6:11, "Give us this day our daily bread." I closed my Bible and waited for his reply.

He looked a bit startled, smiled, and said, "OK." And that was that. We eventually became good friends; in fact he became the faculty sponsor for our Bible study group on campus.

The Bible is very clear. We are called on to share our hearts with the Lord, to call on Him for our needs: "Casting all your care upon Him; for He careth for you" (1 Peter 5:7). Never be afraid to get before God and share your needs, personal concerns, family concerns, things that are often too deep to share with anyone else. These are the things that God as your loving heavenly Father wants to hear from you. He delights to have His children call on His name and share their hurts, telling Him all about their scars and bruises. And constantly He promises to hear and answer. "Whatsoever ye shall ask in My name, that will I do, that the Father may be glorified in the Son. If ye shall ask anything in My name, I will do it" (John 14:13-14). These assurances of answered prayer provide great motivation to seek the Lord's face continually.

He has promised to hear and answer. Daily needs, the difficulties of life that face us, the wisdom we need for decisions that demand attention should all be brought before the Lord on our knees. Prayer is the greatest way I know to demonstrate my dependence on God. My greatest declaration of independence would be to stop praying.

Prayer and Evangelism

I was on a nonstop flight on Malev Airlines aboard a Russian-built jet from Budapest, Hungary to Beirut, Lebanon for some evangelistic meetings in that Middle Eastern city. Hardly anyone else on the plane spoke English, and I was pretty much alone with my thoughts. After the dinner tray had been removed, I turned to the Lord in prayer, for there were many things to pray about that night. The safety of the flight, the spiritual and physical welfare of the family back home, the ongoing and continued fruitfulness of the ministry I had just left in Scotland and England —many things. But as I prayed, one great burden on my heart continued to weigh heavier and heavier as we flew through the night skies. I began to pray for the conversion of a Muslim. I know missionaries who have labored their entire lifetimes in the Middle East without seeing a Muslim come to Christ. But I knew my burden to pray was from the Lord Himself, so I made it a matter of earnest prayer.

Muslims are some of the most difficult people in the world to reach with the Gospel, and the Holy Spirit began to bring passages of Scripture to mind: "Behold, I am the Lord, the God of all flesh; is there anything too hard for Me?" (Jer. 32:27) "Ah, Lord God! Behold, thou hast made the heaven and the earth by Thy great power and stretched-out arm, and there is nothing too hard for Thee" (Jer. 32:17). "Call unto Me, and I will answer thee, and show thee great and mighty things, which thou knowest not" (Jer. 33:3).

These and other passages flooded my mind as we flew through the night. I was encouraged by a letter I had received from the man who was responsible for the meetings in Beirut. He had written: "How are we preparing for this? At this time, 20 people have committed themselves to spend an hour a day and two hours on Saturday in prayer for your time here. This will go on for a month and a half in preparation for your visit." Here are 20 people praying fervently for six weeks prior to the meetings. I had the assurance from God that He was going to do something unusual.

After I had preached the Gospel and given my testimony at a meeting one night, we saw the answer to that prayer. Among those who received Christ was a 25-year-old Muslim. She came up to me the next evening at a rally at one of the universities, and literally glowed with thankfulness and excitement over her new-found faith in the Lord Jesus Christ. Many responded to the message of salvation as a result of those meetings, and the key to it all was prayer.

Linda was a girl who was burdened to pray for one of the members of a very successful and popular singing group in America. This group was the favorite of millions, had made a number of gold records, and drew tremendous crowds wherever they appeared. Year after year she prayed for one of them to come to Christ. Today the person she prayed for travels all over the U.S. performing at concerts and giving his testimony for Christ. I'm sure it was Linda's faithful prayers that were instrumental in this man's conversion.

The Apostle Paul wrote, "Brethren, my heart's desire and prayer to God for Israel is, that they might be saved" (Rom.10:1). I'm sure that you know many people who need the Saviour. Make a list and pray faithfully for them by name. Don't become discouraged if the answer does not come immediately. Keep on praying! "Let us not be weary in well doing, for in due season we shall reap, if we faint not" (Gal. 6:9). God is more concerned for people's salvation than you are. "The Lord is not slack concerning His promise, as some men count slackness; but is long-suffering to us-ward, not willing that any should perish, but that all should come to repentance" (2 Peter 3:9). He waits on us to pray.

Prologue to Chapter 4

Knowing what to do is important. Knowing how to do it is equally important. Knowing what to do, but not knowing how to do it can lead to frustration. Knowing what should be done and refusing or neglecting to do it leads to failure and defeat, because it cuts off the source of strength.

As you begin to spend more and more time in the Word and in prayer, you will need to be open to suggestions as to how to go about continuing and deepening the relationship with your heavenly Father.

In this chapter I want to share some of the lessons God allowed me to learn, and some of the ways I have found useful in keeping the relationship going.

4

The Relationship Deepens

One of the most spectacular revelations in all the Bible is found in the Book of Colossians. In fact, it is called "the mystery which hath been hid from ages and from generations" (Col. 1:26). When I read something like that, my natural curiosity is aroused and I want to be let in on the secret. The next verse in that chapter tells what the mystery is. It is the fact that the Creator of the universe, the Hope of the world, the King of kings, the Lord of lords, the One before whom every knee shall bow, the Person of the Lord Jesus Christ, lives in every Christian. Paul prayed, "That Christ may dwell in your hearts by faith" (Eph. 3:17). How is this great truth to be of practical value to the believer?

Assurance—How to Know You Are a Christian

Tens of thousands of Christians today are believers, but are not sure of their salvation. They've done all they know to do, believed everything they are supposed to believe, but still the assurance that they have been accepted by God into His family is missing. Perhaps you are one of these. Satan would like to keep that truth forever hidden from you. Often he does it by making you doubt your relationship to God.

It is possible to have the assurance. Paul says, "The Spirit [Himself] beareth witness with our spirit, that we are the children of God" (Rom. 8:16). This statement shows that it is possible to know you are a child of God. The Bible gives two evidences of salvation. These do not necessarily come all at once. One may appear, then the other in a slow gradual way. So if you can recognize one or the other of these in your own life, rejoice. You're probably well on the way.

The first is a sincere desire to obey God. John said, "And hereby we do know that we know Him, if we keep His commandments. He that saith, 'I know Him,' and keepeth not His commandments, is a liar, and the truth is not in him" (1 John 2:3-4). You should have a basic desire in your life to obey God. This doesn't mean that you have developed instant, full, complete, immediate obedience in everything at all times. But there will be a growing desire in your heart to be an obedient child of God. Of course, you'll stumble and fall like the rest of us, but there *is* a new hunger to live His way and do His bidding. If so, that's one of the sure signs that the Spirit of God is working in your life.

The other evidence is a genuine love for fellow believers. "If a man say, 'I love God,' and hateth his brother, he is a liar; for he that loveth not his brother, whom he hath seen, how can he love God, whom he hath not seen? And this commandment have we from Him, that he who loveth God love his brother also" (1 John 4:20-21). Again, this may not be fully and completely true at every moment in your life. In other words, you may not love all Christians with a perfect love all of the time. Few of us do. But here's what I think the Apostle John is saying.

As a Christian you should have a growing desire to be more and more involved with the people of God and a lessening of interest in the places and activities of your old crowd of friends. You find greater joy in being with Christians and the things they do. You've discovered that it can be fun to go to a party with Christians and have a good time. You feel great when it's over. One man told me he did not have the letdown when the parties were over that he used to feel before he came to Christ. And he felt *so* much better the next morning! In other words, there is a greater interest developing in your life in the service of Christ and a deepening joy found in fellowship with His followers.

The Apostle John states that the person who finds little or no love in his heart for the family of God, who avoids being with Christians, and who still hungers to run with the old gang because he likes them better and finds them more pleasant to be around, should take a serious look at his own standing before God. He who loves God loves his brother also.

These two evidences burst on the understanding of some Christians quickly. In others, they grow from a faint spark and take months and years to develop. So if you can recognize either of these taking place in your life, take heart. Pray that God's Spirit will continue to bear witness with your spirit and give you the assurance you need to be a growing faithful Christian.

Now obviously I cannot obey God and love fellow Christians if I don't know that I should. Thus I must make it a practice of my life to learn God's Word. Jesus said, "Take my yoke upon you and learn of Me" (Matt. 11:29). Jesus Himself explains how we learn of Him. The Scriptures, He said, "are they which testify of Me" (John 5:39). So we must make sure that we have a daily intake of the Word of God through Bible reading, study, memory, and meditation (see chap. 2).

Growth—How to Grow Spiritually

Often after I've spoken at a meeting, some young guy or gal will come up to me and say, "LeRoy, I want to grow into a strong Christian. Tell me, how can I become mature right away? I've got no time to lose." I usually sit down and try to explain that there is no spiritual tonic they can take, no magic experience they can have that gives them instant growth. There is instant tea and instant coffee, but there is no instant maturity. And it certainly doesn't help to struggle and fret and worry about it. All a person needs to do is meet the conditions for growth and growth occurs at its own pace. It is unstoppable.

I recall the day when we brought Randy, our son, home from the hospital a few days after he was born. He couldn't walk, feed himself, or even focus his eyes. This morning, 17 years later, Randy ate breakfast, walked to the car, and drove off. Not once during those 17 years did he try to grow fast. Like many other kids, he has a place in the bedroom where he occasionally backs up to the wall and marks his growth, but that has come from simply meeting the conditions for growth.

The Apostle Peter admonishes all Christians to "grow in grace and in the knowledge of our Lord and Saviour Jesus Christ" (2 Peter 3:18). To fulfill this command we must satisfy the conditions both in our *inner spirit* and in our *outer performance*.

The first condition to do with our inner attitudes is the necessity of joy. If you're one of those people who comes to breakfast with a scowl and a grumpy mood, you need to memorize Philippians 4:4: "Rejoice in the Lord alway; and again I say, 'Rejoice.' " Ask the Lord to make that truth real to you. If you show up with a cheery good morning and bright smile, I'm sure the bacon, eggs, toast, and coffee will all taste better to you and to everyone else.

Another inner condition is thankfulness. "In everything give thanks, for this is the will of God in Christ Jesus concerning you" (1 Thes. 5:18). Note the words *in everything*. Is that possible? It is, if you believe "that all things work together for good to them that love God, to them who are the called according to His purpose" (Rom. 8:28).

A proper reaction to the storms of life is a must. And isn't it true that a plant growing in the garden needs the rainstorm as well as the sunshine in order for it to grow and produce fruit? God knows just the right amount of sunshine and rain to bring our way so that He might conform us to the image of His Son.

In addition to the inner qualities of joy and thanksgiving, we must have the two outer qualities of discipline and order. Remember, spiritual growth is spiritual *growth*. You must meet the conditions. To grow you need nourishment; your soul must be fed just as your physical body must be fed. And the food for your soul is the Word of God. Paul says, "Let the Word of Christ dwell in you richly in all wisdom, teaching and admonishing one another in psalms and hymns and spiritual songs, singing with grace in your hearts to the Lord" (Col. 3:16).

You must be regular in your feeding on the Word. And with discipline there must be order. If we were disorderly in our physical lives, we would live in the midst of confusion and chaos. Imagine this scene: You come home, throw your coat in the corner, leave magazines and newspapers strewn about, brush your teeth whenever it happens to cross your mind, sleep in your clothes, and never make your bed. Well, that's the way many Christians go about their spiritual lives. Do you have a regular time for Bible study and prayer? Do you have a plan for Scripture memory? Do you have a quiet time with the Lord? If you are to grow you must bring some order and discipline into your spiritual life.

The Will of God—How to Discover It

Christians often wonder what God wants them to do with their lives. We were having a one-day conference at Glen Eyrie, the headquarters of The Navigators, a couple of years ago when I received a phone call from an 87-year-old woman who said she wanted to come, but needed a ride. I told her we would send someone to get her. She then explained, "The reason I want to come is your workshop on how to know the will of God. I've been a Christian since I was a little girl, and I've always wondered about that." After the phone call I thought, *What a tragedy!* Here was a person who had been a Christian for about 80 years, and she had never discovered how to know God's will for her life.

Many Christians don't realize that God has a plan for their lives, and wants to reveal it to them.

In the early '50s Dawson Trotman asked me if I would like to represent The Navigators in the eastern part of the U.S. God had, in fact, given me a desire to work with this group, and Daws told me there were seven places where I could be used. He suggested that I pray about it and see if the Lord gave any direction. I took the matter before the Lord and prayed for many hours; in fact, I prayed through the night. The Lord laid Pittsburgh, one of the cities on the list, on my heart. I went to Daws, told him about it, and he sent me to Pittsburgh. After my arrival I sought the Lord about how to begin the ministry. I spent three weeks alone with God, praying and reading His Word. One day the Lord gave me some verses from 1 Samuel 14. It was unmistakable, point by point, step by step guidance. It became clear that the university was to be the main focal point, and that we would use the approach of presenting the Gospel in the fraternity houses that surrounded the campus.

Shortly after that, Dr. Bill Bright of Campus Crusade for Christ came to the city. The Navigators had loaned me to Crusade to help get their work started in that area. I knew Bill had been mightily used of God on the West Coast and I was full of questions. He answered my questions and taught me by example. The counsel I received from him was invaluable, and has proven so to this day.

After we had been in Pittsburgh for a year, through a series of circumstances, the Lord began to open doors to spread the Gospel at other universities: Penn State, Indiana, Maryland, and others. In reflection, I could see the means God has used to reveal His will to me. Prayer, His Word, godly counsel, and circumstances. And so it is today. God uses these same means to show me His way. "Trust in the Lord with all thine heart, and lean not unto thine own understanding. In all thy ways acknowledge Him, and He shall direct thy paths" (Prov. 3:5-6).

Application—Making the Word of God a Vital Part of Your Life

When I was a young Christian I learned a simple little lesson that has proved to be a rich source of inspiration and help to me through the years. Every morning, I would get my Bible, a notebook, and a pen, and go to a quiet place. I would then open my Bible to the book I had chosen to read. I got on my knees and in earnest prayer asked the Lord to speak to my heart. Then I began to read slowly till in the quietness of my heart of hearts, the Holy Spirit said something just to me. I opened my notebook and wrote it down. Then I began to pray again—praying back to God what He has spoken to my heart.

That was communion with God. From His throne in heaven He had spoken to me by His Holy Spirit through His Word. I had taken that communication and returned it to the throne of grace in prayer. The circle of communion had been completed—from God to me and back to Him. That is a pattern that may also work for you.

Continue to pray on the basis of God's Word to you till your spirit burns with its message. Then take your notebook and jot down some specific plan to put into action that God has placed on your heart. As you write, continue to pray for grace and strength to do what you know you must do. God may speak to you about a command to obey, an example to follow, a sin to forsake, or a promise to claim. Make your application as personal as possible. It will bring spiritual blessing and deepen your relationship to God; it will improve your relationship with fellow Christians and even those outside of Christ. Write down clearly what you intend to do by God's help. It may be memorizing a verse on the subject, so that the Holy Spirit can continue to speak to you; it may be writing a letter to thank someone; it may be a needed apology trying to right some wrong.

If you go to the Bible depending on your human abilities, what you derive will be on the human level. But, if you depend on the Holy Spirit, He will guide you into God's truth. Jesus promised, "When He, the Spirit of truth, is come, He will guide you into all truth; for He shall not speak of Himself, but whatever He shall hear, that shall He speak; and He will show you things to come"

(John 16:13). Your mind by itself can produce more problems than solutions, and lead to frustration and bewilderment, but as you rely on the Holy Spirit, He will bring to your remembrance the very thing you need at the time you need it. "The Comforter [who is the Holy Spirit], whom the Father will send in My name, He shall teach you all things, and bring all things to your remembrance, whatsoever I have said unto you" (John 14:26).

Application is putting the truth of God into practice in daily life. The visible result of time with the Lord is a life being conformed more and more into the image of Christ.

Fellowship—How to Gather Together with Other Christians

Another vital means of keeping Christ at the center of our lives is fellowship. The church provides a means whereby we can assemble with the people of God and find encouragement and strength from the lives of others. Christianity is not a "do it yourself" proposition. We are members one of another, a part of the body of Christ. I've never seen a person live a successful Christian life who neglected the fellowship of those of like precious faith. What a joy it is to gather with other Christians in wonderful fellowship around our Lord Jesus Christ. David said, "I was glad when they said unto me, 'Let us go into the house of the Lord'" (Ps. 122:1).

When you and I were joined to Christ, we were joined to one another. The Bible says, "Now you are together the body of Christ, and individually you are members of Him" (1 Cor. 12:27, PH). Paul also says, "As the human body, which has many parts, is a unity and those parts, despite their multiplicity, constitute one single body, so it is with Christ" (1 Cor. 12:12, PH). Why do you think the Lord did it this way? Well, for one thing, to teach us that we are interdependent. We need each other. We need each other's prayers, encouragement, counsel, and exhortation.

As members of the body of Christ, each one of us has a particular job to do. The Bible says there are different ways of serving, but the same Lord is served (1 Cor. 12:4-6). This means that each one of us has a vital role to play in the life of the church. The body of Christ is like a great mosaic. The picture is complete only as I am in the place where God has put me, doing what He has called me to do, in the way He wants it done.

One of the things I enjoy is building a fire in the fireplace on a cold winter night, staying home with the family, and watching the flames. Fascinating! You may have done this too. Did you ever notice what happens to a live red-hot coal that breaks off from the log and rolls to a corner of the fireplace? Soon it loses its glow and cools off. I've seen people do that as well. They have gotten out of the fellowship, stopped coming to church services, stopped attending the Bible studies or the prayer meetings. They lose their fire and become cold. They lose their glow.

We need the warmth of Christian fellowship to maintain our vital walk and witness for Christ. We need each other. Have you ever noticed the way the Holy Spirit refers to the fellowship of the early believers in the Book of Acts? "The multitude of them that believed were of one heart and of one soul" (Acts 4:32). We find these words repeated: One heart, one soul, one mind, one spirit. Or take the phrase *one accord*. It appears 13 times in the Bible (KJV), 11 of which are in the Book of Acts.

Did you know that the word *love* never appears in Acts? You see, these are not the meditations of the apostles, but the acts. They demonstrated their love by living in one accord, with one heart, one mind, one soul. The result? "With great power gave the apostles witness of the resurrection of the Lord Jesus; and great grace was upon them all" (Acts 4:33).

I enjoy fellowship and Bible study with others. The most profitable way I have found is for each member of the group to study a portion of Scripture for a week or so, and then meet to share what the Lord has taught us. Another means of vital fellowship is to meet and pray together. I've met in early morning prayer meetings with men, and we've prayed about our families, our work, friends who need Christ, financial needs—all those things that make up the normal affairs of life.

I've met with other Christians in prayer and have gone out into the neighborhoods to share Christ as the Lord opened up opportunities. This really drew our hearts together as we were out in the battle. Christian fellowship is a blessed means of growth and a source of joy to our lives.

Witness—How to Share Christ with Others
Finally, when Christ is in the center, there is an overflow of spiritual blessings into the lives of others. Witnessing is a natural outcome of this kind of life, resulting from a deep commitment to

Christ as Lord, daily time with Him in the Word and prayer, a heart that responds in obedience to His voice, and a vital fellowship with other Christians.

Quite often we evaluate our witnessing and determine to do better, or become angry with ourselves for our neglect of sharing Christ. This does little good. Witnessing is in a real sense the barometer of our lives that tells how the other aspects of our walk with Christ are getting along. Jesus dwells in our lives and wants to be the center of all that we are and all that we do. When we allow Him that central place on the throne of our hearts, the Spirit of God floods our lives with the peace and joy that only He can bring.

Prologue to Chapter 5

Since the day of your birth, you have been doing what you want to do—in a sense, being your own god. You have served yourself, worshiped yourself, and promoted your own ends and interests. Now you are a Christian and all that has changed.

A new life has begun for you, but old self-centered thought patterns are hard to break. Self clings tenaciously to the throne of your heart and becomes a hard tenant to evict. But the fact remains that for the Christian, Jesus is Lord, and He must be so, not only because Scripture says so, but in our daily lives as well.

This chapter speaks to the theme of the Lordship of Christ. I believe you will find, as I and millions of others have, that as you allow Him to be your Lord, it is not a grievous responsibility, but something that you really enjoy. I can assure you, it's really great to work for a Master who knows what He's doing, and One who takes such good care of His servants.

5

The Lordship of Christ

The Bible says of Jesus: "He is Lord of all" (Acts 10:36). His name *Jesus* means that He is our Saviour, "Thou shalt call His name Jesus, for He shall save His people from their sins" (Matt. 1:21). *Christ* means that He is the anointed Holy One of God, God's only begotten Son. To say *Lord* presupposes obedience on our part. Jesus asks, "And why call ye Me, 'Lord, Lord,' and do not the things which I say?" (Luke 6:46) He also declares, "Ye call Me Master and Lord, and ye say well, for so I am" (John 13:13). Note well: He is our master, our teacher and our Lord; He is to be obeyed.

The Central Issue

One day Jesus and His disciples were in a small boat during a great storm. He was asleep in the back of the boat and His disciples woke Him and cried, "Master, carest Thou not that we perish?" He awoke "and rebuked the wind, and said unto the sea, 'Peace, be still.' And the wind ceased, and there was a great calm. And they feared exceedingly, and said one to another, 'What manner of Man is this, that even the wind and the sea obey Him?' " (Mark 4:38-39, 41) What manner of Man indeed? The Master of nature's elements.

On another occasion Jesus was called to the house of Lazarus, who had been dead four days. Jesus went to the tomb and cried with a loud voice, "Lazarus, come forth!" Immediately, "he that was dead came forth, bound hand and foot with graveclothes, and his face was bound about with a napkin. Jesus saith unto them, 'Loose him, and let him go' " (John 11:43-44). Jesus has power over death! What manner of Man is this? The Master of life.

Another time Jesus met a man who was demon-possessed. This man "had his dwelling among the tombs; and no man could bind him, no, not with chains; because that he had been often bound with fetters and chains, and the chains had been plucked asunder by him, and the fetters broken in pieces; neither could any man tame him. And always, night and day, he was in the mountains, and in the tombs, crying and cutting himself with stones. . . . And [Jesus] asked him, 'What is thy name?' And he answered, saying, 'My name is Legion, for we are many' " (Mark 5:3-5, 9). Here was a man whom the devil had in his grip, a man possessed with thousands of demons from hell. Jesus had compassion on him, and cast the demons out to set the man free. He has power over the demons of hell. What manner of Man is this? The Master of even the spirit world. The Apostle Peter summed it up: "He is the Lord of all" (Acts 10:36).

The central issue, however, is whether or not Jesus Christ is Lord of my life, and whether I have submitted my will to Him. His words to the disciples confront all of us: "If any man will come after Me, let him deny himself, and take up his cross daily and follow Me" (Luke 9:23). Paul explains what it means to give up all rights to myself: "The love of Christ constraineth us; because we thus judge, that if one died for all, then were all dead; and that He died for all, that they which live should not henceforth live unto themselves, but unto Him which died for them, and rose again" (2 Cor. 5:14-15).

We should not live for ourselves, nor should we live for the sins and pleasures and froth and tinsel and the empty praise of the world. "Love not the world, neither the things that are in the world. If any man love the world, the love of the Father is not in Him. For all that is in the world, the lust of the flesh, and the lust of the eyes, and the pride of life, is not of the Father, but is of the world. And the world passeth away, and the lust thereof, but he that doeth the will of God abideth forever" (1 John 2:15-17). And Paul said, "If ye then be risen with Christ, seek those things which are above, where Christ sitteth on the right hand of God. Set your affection on things above, not on things on the earth. For ye are dead, and your life is hid with Christ in God" (Col. 3:1-3).

You see, when we are born into the kingdom of God, there is a King over us. Jesus Christ is that King—the King of kings and the Lord of lords.

How do I know if Christ is the Lord of my life? One thing I can do is to look at my check stubs. What do I spend my money on? On myself? How do I spend my time? What pleasures do I enjoy? Worldly things that draw me away from the Lord? What is my attitude toward Him regarding fellowship in the Word and in prayer? Do I take a soft attitude toward sin just to make people like me or accept me?

If Christ has not been your Lord in practice, you may need to pray a prayer of repentance to God. Thank Him for forgiving you so freely: "If we confess our sins, He is faithful and just to forgive us our sins, and to cleanse us from all unrighteousness" (1 John 1:9). You can start all over, fresh, clean. You can purpose today to make Jesus Christ the Lord of your life, to follow, obey, trust, and love Him. You can commit yourself to Him by praying: "Lord Jesus, today I give my heart and life to You. I commit myself to You as my Master and Lord. In response to your call, 'My son, give Me thine heart,' I give my heart to You."

With Jesus, obedience to the Father was a way of life. He said, "I came down from heaven, not to do Mine own will, but the will of Him that sent Me" (John 6:38). Toward the end of His ministry Jesus said, "As My Father hath sent Me, even so send I you" (John 20:21). To the one who makes obedience a way of life, Jesus makes a promise: "He that hath My commandments, and keepeth them, he it is that loveth Me; and he that loveth Me shall be loved of My Father, and I will love him, and will manifest Myself to him" (John 14:21). Jesus reveals Himself to the obedient heart. What a promise! Love responds to love. The psalmist said, "Blessed are they that keep His testimonies" (Ps. 119:2). As we obey God's Word, it will keep us right in our thinking, warm in our spirit, and holy in conversation. Doing what we know is God's will gives us peace in our hearts.

Becoming More Like Jesus

An old hymn that we don't hear very much any more goes something like this: "Be like Jesus, this my song, / In the home and in the throng; / Be like Jesus, all day long, / I would be like Jesus." James Rowe, who wrote the words, was surely on the right track. The Bible says, "Whom He did foreknow, He also did predestinate to be conformed to the image of His Son, that He might be the firstborn among many brethren" (Rom. 8:29).

God's purpose for us is that we might be conformed to the image of His Son. The Bible also says we "are constantly being transfigured into His very own image in ever increasing splendor and from one degree of glory to another; [for this comes] from the Lord [Who is] the Spirit" (2 Cor. 3:18, AMP). Here are two important lessons. It is the Holy Spirit of God who accomplishes this in our lives, and it is a process, a gradual life-changing transformation. We are like a baby when we're born into the family of God. Now a baby is complete—five toes on each foot, two ears, two eyes, ten fingers, and so on. He is complete but he must grow. As we grow spiritually we are transformed more and more into Christ's likeness.

If there was ever a time in history when the world needs the powerful influence of the life of Christ, it is today. Praise God, you and I can have that influence. In fact, that might be the most important thing you will ever do with your life. What is it that you can do to become more Christ-like? Jesus told us to learn of Him. In practical terms, what does that mean? If you were to set out to do that on a vigorous program for the next six months, what would you do?

For one thing, you could decide to live in the four Gospels for a while. Make it a special project to read Matthew, Mark, Luke, and John over and over again. The first time through jot down everything you notice about Jesus' prayer life. When did He pray? How long did He pray? What did He pray about? As you jot things down ask the Lord to work those things into your life.

When you complete that project, read those four books again. This time jot down everything you see about how Jesus talked to people about His Father in heaven. What did He say about heaven? What is the way to get there? Is there a hell? Then after you have finished that project, go through the Gospels again and look for His attitudes toward and use of the Word of God. Did He have confidence in the Word? How did He use the Word? How did He refer to the Scripture? These are just a few ideas that you might be able to use.

You wouldn't want to read just the Gospels for too long because you must remember that "all Scripture is given by inspiration of God, and is profitable for doctrine, for reproof, for correction, for instruction in righteousness" (2 Tim. 3:16). Scripture is useful . . .

- for doctrine—what to believe or claim for yourself.
- for reproof—what to forsake or stop doing.
- for correction—what to improve on or do better.
- for instruction—what to learn to begin doing.

The New Testament is full of valuable information about the Lord Jesus that is so applicable to us today. For instance, how do you react to criticism? Do you bristle? Do you justify your actions or answer back with a heated argument? What did Jesus do? "When He was reviled, [He] reviled not again; when He suffered, He threatened not; but committed Himself to Him that judgeth righteously" (1 Peter 2:23). He didn't answer back. He merely committed the matter to His Father in heaven.

I was in Rod Sargent's office one day taking care of some matters. Rod is a vice-president of The Navigators. A person came into Rod's office while I was there and criticized him unnecessarily for something that had happened in the work. This went on and on. Finally he stormed out of Rod's office and the two of us were left alone.

I turned to Rod and asked him why he had taken that, because both he and I knew that he was in no way responsible.

Rod smiled and said, "Well, LeRoy, these things are settled in heaven." He didn't criticize back, but committed the matter to God.

My first reaction was, "Rod's a big man." But upon reflection I say, "Rod did the thing Jesus did." Note what Peter said, "For what glory is it, if, when ye be buffeted for your faults, ye shall take it patiently? But if, when ye do well, and suffer for it, ye take it patiently, this is acceptable with God" (1 Peter 2:20).

Look at another aspect of the life of Christ. How did He look on the idea of serving rather than being served? Here was the King of kings in our midst. Did He demand the rights of a king? Not at all, for He said, "Even the Son of man came not to be ministered unto, but to minister, and to give His life a ransom for many" (Mark 10:45). What did He teach His disciples? "Jesus called them unto Him, and said, 'Ye know that the princes of the Gentiles exercise dominion over them, and they that are great exercise authority upon them. But it shall not be so among you; but whosoever will be great among you, let him be your minister; and whosoever will be chief among you, let him be your servant' " (Matt. 20:25-27).

Now then, in light of all that, when the weather is hot and muggy, it is much easier to wait for the other person to bring the iced tea rather than for us to get up and serve him, isn't it? Time spent in the presence of Jesus in fellowship through the Word and prayer would change all that.

The secret is to spend a good deal of time in fellowship with the Saviour, for when you spend much time with a person, you begin to take on his attitudes and mannerisms.

Having the Right Heart Attitude
When you examine the life of Christ you might be tempted to look at yourself and say, "How can God ever use a person like me? I sin, I fail, and then sin again. I feel like giving it all up." Do you ever feel like that? From Psalm 119:3 we read these words: "They also do no iniquity; they walk in His ways." Do you read verses like that and feel just like throwing in the towel?

I remember the day I almost did just that. I was so fed up with myself and I saw those statements like "they also do no iniquity" and wondered if maybe I was just not cut out for this Christian life. The Christian life seemed to work for others but I just couldn't seem to make a go of it. Others seemed to be living in victory and walking with the Lord, but that sure wasn't the case with me. Was there something basically wrong with me? Surely, there was more to the Christian life than this.

Well, there *was* something wrong, and the thing that was wrong was my understanding of Scripture. Psalm 119:3 and others, like, "Little children, let no man deceive you; he that doeth righteousness is righteous, even as He is righteous. He that committeth sin is of the devil. . . . Whosoever is born of God doth not commit sin" (1 John 3:7-9).

Then a Bible teacher came along who pointed out a beautiful truth that has really helped me. He pointed out that these verses simply describe the heart attitude of the person who desires to walk in God's ways: For instance, they do not live for sin; they do not delight in sin; they do not continue in sin as a way of life. Naturally, they will slip from the path occasionally; that is the nature of a sheep, and that's what we are in the sight of God. He is the Good Shepherd and we are the sheep of His pasture.

Jesus said of Himself, "And when He putteth forth His own sheep, He goeth before them, and the sheep follow Him, for they know His voice. . . . I am the Good Shepherd; the Good Shepherd giveth His life for the sheep. . . . My sheep hear My voice, and I know them, and they follow Me; and I give unto them eternal life; and they shall never perish, neither shall any man pluck them out of My hand" (John 10:4, 11, 27-28).

A sheep is a very dumb animal and prone to wander. Because we are sheep, life cannot be all that complicated. Had He referred to us as foxes, wily and clever, maybe it would have been different. We are not clever foxes, but wayward sheep, and to succeed in life we need to have it made pretty simple. And it is. God says, "Obey Me, and be sorry when you don't. Confess your sins, get back on the track, and follow Me." Isn't that a beautiful picture? Jesus, the Good Shepherd leading His people to the safety of the fold, caring for them, protecting them, loving them, and dying for them.

Following Jesus, that Great Shepherd of the sheep, is the path of purity of life. Why? Perhaps you've never noticed it before, but the psalmist said, "He leadeth me in the paths of righteousness for His name's sake" (Ps. 23:3). So if you have fallen into the trap of struggling for holiness and purity of life, then realize that it doesn't come that way. It is by surrender, not struggle. Learn to walk with Jesus in daily fellowship with Him. He will lead you in paths of righteousness, for He is more concerned about your welfare than you are, because you belong to Him.

Following the Shepherd's Voice
In the Holy Land one Friday we had walked from Jerusalem's sheep gate up to the sheep market. It was a fascinating sight: shepherds buying and selling, some coming to settle their differences or enjoying each other's company. One man was sitting on a powerful white horse, recounting the ancestry of his steed for the past 200 years. As we were leaving, we saw a very strange

sight. We had seen hundreds of sheep calmly following the shepherds, but here was a sheep lunging and leaping and straining to break away from the rope that a shepherd was using to lead it along. All the other sheep were gentle and quiet. But not this one. It was throwing itself against the stone wall, jerking, and trying to pull away.

Our guide called our attention to it and asked if we knew the reason for its strange behavior. We were fascinated by what we saw, but couldn't figure out the reason. The answer, our guide said, was in the Bible: "A stranger will they [sheep] not follow, but will flee from him; for they know not the voice of strangers" (John 10:5). The answer was simple. This shepherd had just purchased the sheep, and the sheep knew he was in the hands of a stranger, so it would not follow him.

Today the voice of strangers is heard everywhere, calling Christians to leave the straight and narrow path and follow the way of the world, the broad way that leads to destruction. The Bible says, "There is a way that seemeth right unto a man but the end thereof are the ways of death" (Prov. 16:25). I have talked to hundreds of people who have told me that their experience in following the way of the world, the flesh, and the devil led them into frustration, guilt, depression, alienation from God, unhappiness, and emptiness of life.

I know we often speak of the dumb sheep, but as I watched that sheep trying to remain with the shepherd that it knew and trusted, I realized that in that regard it was pretty smart. When you realize you have strayed, there are two things you need to do. One is to get back on the right track. The other is to stay there. Quite often men and women have asked me, "LeRoy, how do you make it over the long haul? How can I be sure that I'm still on track 25 years from now?"

The answer is simple. The way you make it over the long haul is to follow Jesus today.

Today is all you've got. Yesterday is gone. Tomorrow never comes. So today, walk with Him, stay in the Word, keep your prayer life in order. Deny yourself the urge to do your own thing and instead do what you know is right. Follow the instructions Barnabas gave the new Christians in Antioch, when he "exhorted them all, that with purpose of heart they would cleave unto the Lord" (Acts 11:23).

The Burning Bush

People in the Holy Land appreciate a certain bush that grows there. It is small, grows close to the ground and, if you look closely, has the appearance of chicken wire. Our guide told us it was used by the people as fuel. It is also used as a fence to keep the small animals penned in.

After examining the plant I asked our guide what it was called. I was surprised to learn that the people call it "the burning bush." They use it in their ovens to bake their bread. It is plentiful, and burns a long time with a hot flame. It was then that I remembered the experience of Moses. Imagine seeing one of those little bushes on fire and not being consumed. When it happened to Moses, he said, "I will now turn aside, and see this great sight, why the bush is not burnt" (Ex. 3:3).

I know some people like the bush Moses saw. My wife, Virginia, has a Bible study with a group of women each week. Ann, a participant in that study, is one of the most cheerful and victorious women I've ever met, even though she has been blind for eight years. She has diabetes, is on a kidney dialysis machine three times a week, and her potassium count often rises to such a level that it stops her heart. She hovers at the brink of death, and undergoes tremendous physical suffering, but her cheery and radiant spirit has caused many doctors and nurses to take notice. They marvel that, though her life has undergone the fires of pain and suffering for years, her spirit is not consumed.

My mother had the same kind of spirit. She lived on the edge of poverty most of her life. She wore hand-me-down clothes. Her third son had cerebral palsy for years and died in his late 30s. Many a day she had to send her husband and sons off to work with sauerkraut sandwiches in their lunchboxes. Yet the thing I remember about her is her cheery spirit. When she baked bread, and it was the best bread in the county, she would always bake an extra loaf or two. Then she would put it in a sack, give it to me with instructions to take it to some friends who were having difficulties. "It may cheer them up a little bit," she'd say.

For years she endured the fires of poverty and heartache; yet she was not consumed. In fact, she spent much of her life trying to figure out ways to bring cheer and happiness to others. Though she was a tiny little woman, she was big, because you can always tell the size of a person by what it takes to get him down. I think it would have taken a herd of elephants to crush her. Why are some people like that?

I think it has to do with the basic approach to life. You either live for yourself or for others.

A person who is all wrapped up in himself has his mind turned inward. He is more concerned about the right after-shave lotion than the earthquake in Chile. Frankly, only Christ can change his attitude, because He lived for others from the beginning. Jesus left the glories of heaven for the grime and grief of earth. He spent His life doing good. He suffered in Gethsemane and endured the scourging of whips and the crown of thorns for others.

He died on the cross for the sins of others. He lives today at the right hand of God as a mediator for others.

A life lived in vital union with Him is the secret of a radiant life lived in the midst of suffering and heartache. He said, "He that loveth his life shall lose it; and he that hateth his life in this world shall keep it unto life eternal. If any man serve Me, let him follow Me; and where I am, there shall also My servant be. If any man serve Me, him will My Father honor" (John 12:25-26).

Joy in Obedience

The happy man is the obedient man. The man who disobeys the Word of God does not find freedom but disaster, pain, trouble, and heartbreak. Keeping God's law will do more for us than all the morals of the philosophers and the customs of society. People err in two ways: by living by no rules and by living by the wrong rules. Happiness comes only by living by God's rules.

Some say, "I'll make up my own rules, my own standards." The major problem is that it won't work. That philosophy only leads to chaos and disaster. Think of an athlete about to run a race asking, "How long is the race? 220 meters? 440 meters?"

The official replies, "I don't know."

"Which way is the finish line?"

"Just run in whatever direction you want," says the official.

It wouldn't be much of a race, would it? Yet some would have us live like that: no standards, no absolutes, only doing what you want.

Jesus said, "Whosoever cometh to Me, and heareth My sayings, and doeth them . . . is like a man which built an house, and digged deep, and laid the foundation on a rock. . . . But he that heareth, and doeth not, is like a man that without a foundation built an house upon the earth, against which the stream did beat vehemently, and immediately it fell, and the ruin of that house was great" (Luke 6:47-49).

Three reasons for living in obedience to God are:

1. It is necessary for fellowship, because there is no fellowship with a superior apart from obedience. When the sergeant says, "Forward, march!" and the private replies, "Hang it on your beak," they have just lost their fellowship (plus the private may end up in the brig). The Bible says, "If we say that we have fellowship with Him, and walk in darkness, we lie, and do not the truth; but if we walk in the light, as He is in the light, we have fellowship one with another, and the blood of Jesus Christ His Son cleanseth us from all sin" (1 John 1:6-7).

2. It is necessary for an effective prayer life. "Whatsoever we ask, we receive of Him, because we keep His commandments, and do those things that are pleasing in His sight" (1 John 3:22).

3. It brings glory to God. What is our main purpose in life? "Let your light so shine before men, that they may see your good works, and glorify your Father which is in heaven" (Matt. 5:16).

The Valley of Elah

While I was visiting the Holy Land, I saw something in the valley of Elah that reminded me of another important lesson about Christ's Lordship. Shepherds still go to the brook that flows in that valley to find smooth stones for their goat-hair slings. These shepherds are incredibly accurate with their slings, and they choose rocks to fit the situations: for example, a large one for a bear, a smaller one for a partridge. As I leaned down and picked up a stone from the water, I thought of David.

"Saul and the men of Israel were gathered together, and pitched by the valley of Elah, and set the battle in array against the Philistines, and the Philistines stood on a mountain on the one side, and Israel stood on a mountain on the other side; and there was a valley between them" (1 Sam. 17:2-3). Goliath, the Philistine giant, came and threw out the challenge: "I defy the armies of Israel this day; give me a man, that we may fight together" (17:10).

In the meantime, David the shepherd boy had come to bring food for his brothers, but when he heard the challenge he volunteered to go and fight the giant. "And David said to Saul, 'Let no man's heart fail because of him; thy servant will go and fight with this Philistine. . . . David said moreover, 'The Lord that delivered me out of the paw of the lion and out of the paw of the bear, He will deliver me out of the hand of this Philistine.' And Saul said unto David, 'Go, and the Lord be with thee.' . . . And he took his staff in his hand, and chose him five smooth stones out of the brook, and put them in a shepherd's bag which he had . . . and his sling was in his hand, and he drew near to the Philistine.

"And the Philistine said unto David, 'Am I a dog that thou comest to me with staves?' And the Philistine cursed David by his gods. . . . [And David said], 'All this assembly shall know that the Lord saveth not with sword and spear; for the battle is the Lord's, and He will give you into our hands.' . . . And David put his hand in his bag, and took thence a stone and slang it, and smote the Philistine in his forehead, that the stone sunk into his forehead; and he fell upon his face to the earth. So David prevailed over the Philistine with a sling and with a stone, and smote the Philistine, and slew him; but there was no sword in the hand of David" (1 Sam. 17:32-50).

Two great lessons burst from this story. One, the lesson of faith. This was basically a spiritual battle. The Philistine cursed David by his gods and David said, "I come to thee in the name of the Lord of hosts . . . that all the earth may know there is a God in Israel" (1 Sam. 17:45-46). We all need to learn that lesson. The giants in our lives can be overcome by the power of God—the giants of fear, doubt, pride, and anxiety that come to us day by day and challenge us to mortal combat. We must go forth in the name of God and in His strength.

The other lesson is equally powerful. Too often we say to ourselves, I could do something great for God if I had that person's abilities or this person's talents. We feel sorry for ourselves and make up excuses as to why we are not doing more for the Lord. But at the Valley of Elah, David taught us an eternal and powerful lesson. He did what he could with what he had. Though it was only a simple goat-hair sling and a few rocks from the brook, he used it to win the victory. The Lord calls on all of us to do the same. The Spirit of God has given every man gifts that He chose for him. We are to make do with what we've been given. And we can only do that when Christ is Lord in our lives.

Prologue to Chapter 6

It is the life of a Christian that speaks volumes. A life of joy, peace, and fulfillment is a thing of beauty in a world filled with sad people, lacking peace and purpose. Jesus said, "Let your light so shine before men, that they may see your good works, and glorify your Father which is in heaven" (Matt. 5:16).

As you grow in discipleship, what you are in the eyes of your friends will speak louder than what you say. As a growing disciple, your life will be watched by those around you, and will be used of God to draw others to Himself.

More and more, as you continue to walk with the Lord you will see that what you are, or what you appear to be on the outside will be shallow and meaningless unless it reflects the kind of Christian character the Lord wants to develop within you. This is the true meaning of discipleship.

6

Discipleship—Living Under the Lordship of Christ

In the last chapter we saw what the Lordship of Christ means. We now need to see what effect His Lordship should have on our lives. A person who is under Jesus' Lordship will reflect certain character traits. They will be visible to all.

Discipline

Perhaps one of the most important character traits in a Christian living under the Lordship of Christ is discipline.

I was in Annapolis one summer and decided to go and see three fellows whom I had known over the years. Two of them were graduates of the Naval Academy, the other had graduated from the Air Force Academy in Colorado Springs. They had rented an apartment in that Navy town and were participating in a Navigators summer training program.

I walked into their apartment unannounced and when the three fellows saw me they shouted in startled surprise, "LeRoy!" For four years these men had been the apex of neatness and order. Their uniforms were neat and pressed at all times. Their rooms were clean and orderly, with everything in its place. In the academies beds are made to rigid specifications, clothing is hung just so, shoes are shined and in place. It's quite a contrast to what you see in the average university dormitory in America.

Now here were these three academy grads with the most sheepish looks on their faces that I had ever seen. They were chagrined and ill at ease. They stood in the middle of the biggest mess on earth. The beds were unmade; shoes, socks, shirts, pants, underwear, coats, and jackets were strewn about the room; dirty dishes filled the sink; dust covered the furniture and shelves.

I looked around and said, "Wow, guys! I'm sorry I missed the brawl. Who won?" I smiled, which seemed to put them somewhat at ease, and then we had some fellowship. The situation was easy to figure out. Here were men who for four years had discipline imposed on them, and now they were enjoying their freedom. They could put anything anywhere or nowhere; it didn't matter.

I'm sure it comes as no surprise to you that the word *discipline* and *disciple* are related. But the Bible does not say that a disciple is one who is under some external pressure and is forced to live a certain way. The motivation of the disciple is not external, but from within.

A few years ago my wife was going through a spiritual dry spell. She began to pray that she would have a sense of the presence of God and a hunger to spend time alone with Him in the Word and in prayer. As a result of those prayers, she now finds great joy and delight in meeting with the Lord in the early morning hours. She can hardly wait for the alarm to go off at 5 A.M. She bounds out of bed, heads for the kitchen table with her Bible and prayer list, and spends about two and a half hours with the Lord. It isn't something she *has* to do. No one is forcing her. She is not under some artificial external pressure. She *wants* to. The desire is in her heart. And that is the discipline of a disciple of Christ.

The Power of Love
In this age we hear a lot about power—hydroelectrical power, nuclear power, black power, presidential power. We have become so dependent on it that when power fails it can bring tragedy. The Bible speaks of an unfailing power source in this world. The Apostle Paul said, "Love never fails" (1 Cor. 13:8, AMP).

One of the newer translations of this passage puts it this way: "This love of which I speak is slow to lose patience—it looks for ways of being constructive. It is not possessive: it is neither anxious to impress nor does it cherish inflated ideas of its own importance. Love has good manners and does not pursue selfish advantage. It is not touchy. It does not keep account of evil or gloat over the wickedness of other people. On the contrary, it is glad with all good men when truth prevails. Love knows no limits to its endurance, no end to its trust, no fading of its hope; it can outlast anything. It is, in fact, the one thing that still stands when all else has fallen. . . . In this life we have three great lasting qualities—faith, hope and love. But the greatest of them is love" (1 Cor. 13:4-8, 13, PH). What a beautiful statement to the enduring power of love!

One day when my son Randy was in elementary school, he came home and announced that the teacher had them write a definition of love. I became quite interested and asked the little guy what he had written.

He shuffled his feet and looked down at the floor and said, "Well, Dad, it wasn't very much." When I told him I'd sure like to know what he had said, he replied, "To love is to give."

I was amazed. "Man," I told him, "that's great. Where did you come up with such a great definition?"

He looked surprised. "Dad," he said, "haven't you ever seen John 3:16?" I looked at him with profound respect. He had hit the nail right on the head. God so loved the world that He gave.

When the New Testament was written there were a number of Greek words that expressed the idea of love. It is highly significant that the word meaning "personal desire" or "self-seeking" does not even occur. There are two words translated *love* that do appear. One is human love, the love that is given by a person in return for love offered to that person. However, the word that appears most frequently is a love that gives itself without counting the cost and does not depend on the merits of the other person. It is the divine love that only God can enable us to express. But love which the world sings about, writes about, and makes movies about is the word that does not even appear in the New Testament. No wonder the world is filled with disenchanted people.

A few years ago a popular song told us, "What the world needs now is love. That's the only thing there's just too little of." I agree, if they are talking about the real thing. But all too often, love is not spelled "g-i-v-e"; it is spelled "t-a-k-e" or "l-u-s-t." There lies the problem. The Word of God is our source of truth on this topic, but most people ignore it. God is love, and to truly understand love, we must get to know Him.

The Teachable Heart
When a pastor or a fellow Christian comes to you and says,

"Friend, I'd like to tell you that you have something in your life that will prove deadly if you let it continue," what is your reaction? Many would say, "Who is he to try to talk to me about this thing? I'm just as good as he is. I've got lots of good points. Why doesn't he notice those? Why is he picking on me about this?" If responses like these arise, take a look at God's Word: "I will praise Thee with uprightness of heart, when I shall have learned Thy righteous judgments" (Ps. 119:7). The word *learned* implies the humility to learn, from anybody, from any situation. A teachable heart is the mark of a truly big man or woman.

I recall an instance when Dawson Trotman was admonishing us to keep our hearts open and learn from others. "You can even learn from the devil," he told us.

I remember being somewhat startled, and I suppose I showed it.

"Well," he said. "Think how the devil is so diligent in his follow-up of a new Christian. When a person comes to Christ, quite often someone from a false cult calls on him, or an old girl-friend shows up, or he gets a job offer where he has to work during the time the Bible study meets, and so on." Think how often we've done something dumb and then tried to justify it rather than just admit we were wrong and learn from it.

Pride is often the reason we don't like to admit that certain things we've done are wrong, or that the way we do certain things could be improved. You will never be a true disciple of Jesus Christ if you have that spirit, because the very word *disciple* means "learner." The person who knows all he needs to know, who resents a word of admonition or correction, has stopped learning.

If the person giving you the suggestion feels that you resent his counsel, he may well hesitate to give it again, and you have lost a valuable source of help. So the next time someone shows enough concern for you to mention an area of your life that needs strengthening, respond with joy and thankfulness because often we can't see our own faults and need the guidance and help of others. I've met people in their 70s who are bright-eyed, have an inquisitive spirit, and are living on the edge of life, right out where things are happening. And I've also met people who are recently out of college and who have already started to dry up in their intellectual lives. That's a tragedy.

Don't let life shrivel up around you. Keep the door of learning open.

Joy, Even in Difficulty

I've been in two airports that were shut down—Heathrow in London during the summer of 1974, and O'Hare in Chicago in the spring of 1975. I can tell you, it's not a pleasant experience. Many frustrated and angry people have many places to go, but have no way to get there and nothing to do. And you see many strange things.

In London the problem was caused by the people who fuel the planes. Without warning, they just walked off and went on strike. It was at the height of the holiday season for people who live in Great Britain. Thousands of people flooded into the airport, and very few went out.

At O'Hare the problem was caused by a spring snow. For the third time in its history, O'Hare was completely shut down—nothing came in or out for about 24 hours. People's nerves became raw. I stopped in one of the quickie coffee shops to get something to eat. A man working behind the counter was screaming at an employee, "Don't you criticize me. I won't have you coming in here and talking to me that way." He had lost all control.

I walked over to the Airport Hotel to try to find a telephone that was not being used. There was a man on one phone cursing at the top of his lungs. He was obviously rich, influential, and powerful, but there he was just like everybody else, helpless. His money and influence couldn't do a thing for him. So, the only thing he could do was swear. People were sleeping everywhere—on the floor, in the baggage area, sitting in chairs. One man told me there were 17 people in his hotel room.

In the midst of it all, I saw a strange sight: a man walking along, *singing*. With anger, frustration, cursing, and raw nerves all around him, this man was just bubbling with happiness and joy. I went up to him and said, "You seem happy. What have you got that gives you happiness and joy in the midst of all this?"

"I am happy," he replied. "I'm one of those who know Jesus Christ as my personal Saviour and Lord."

I smiled and said, "I thought so." With that introduction, we then had a time of fellowship together in the Lord.

If *your* Christian life doesn't reflect joy you should take an inventory to see if the joy-producing means of grace are being neglected: the Word, fellowship with others in worship, or possibly your prayer life.

Balance—Spiritual and Physical

In many areas of life if you lose your balance, you're in trouble. When we were kids we used to go down to the local stockyards and play tag. We would run along the tops of the partitions that separated the pens, swing on the gates and hand-over-hand on the beams that stretched from one side to the other. It was lots of fun, but if someone lost his balance and fell to the ground, he became "it." Then he had to start chasing everybody else.

The basketball player who has one shot to win the game in the playoffs and is forced to shoot while he is off balance will likely miss the shot. In boxing, balance is a must. The fighter who gets off balance is an easy match for his opponent. In most sports, balance is a key to performing well.

So it is in the Christian life. The Scriptures give us an interesting insight into Jesus' early years: "Jesus increased in wisdom and stature, and in favor with God and man" (Luke 2:52). Here are four areas of growth in the life of our Lord: Intellectual, physical, spiritual, and social.

The intellectual aspect is stressed from your youth. You are encouraged by your parents, teachers, aunts, uncles, friends, grandmother and grandfather, to study hard in school. When you learn to read or write your name, it's a big event. The Bible certainly expects the development of the mind. Much of the Book of Proverbs is devoted to the definition of wisdom, knowledge, and understanding, and how to get them.

The social side of life isn't really all that difficult if a couple of things are kept clearly in mind. As a new Christian, I found myself completely at a loss because I didn't know the language, hymns, and accepted behavior patterns. The Lord in His grace gave me a couple of Scriptures that I memorized and prayed over for months. Gradually they had their effect. They were: "A merry heart doeth good like a medicine; but a broken spirit drieth the bones" (Prov. 17:22); "A man that hath friends must show himself friendly: and there is a friend that sticketh closer than a brother" (Prov. 18:24). I asked God to make me a cheerful, friendly person who could be at ease around people.

The physical life must be vigorously maintained. It is so easy to become soft and flabby, to lose your health and vigor. Proper rest, diet, and exercise are the keys to it. Most people need about eight hours rest each night. Staying up late does two things: limits your time with God in the morning, and makes you feel lousy the next day. Lorne Sanny, president of The Navigators, has a regular bedtime, and he won't violate it unless he is in the process of leading a person to Christ.

Proper diet, with a balance of protein, fats, and carbohydrates, isn't hard to get in this land of plenty. In fact, the people who study these things tell us that our chief enemy is not eating too much but not enough of the right foods.

About 15 years ago I had headaches almost every day, and I was always tired and listless. I was easy prey for most of the bugs that went around—colds, flu, whatever. I had no idea what was wrong with me. I had listened to a man in Minneapolis talk about the devil, and I began to wonder if I was under some sort of satanic attack. One day the local Young Life director invited me to go with him to the gym for a workout. I declined. Years ago I had given up all forms of exercise because of a wound in my left knee during World War II. I thought the only exercises were the running sports—baseball, football, basketball. Because I couldn't do these things anymore, I assumed all exercise was out. But Dick assured me that they had equipment down there that I could use, get a good workout, and not hurt my knee one bit. So I took his word for it and decided to go.

Dick was right. I soon discovered exercises that gave me a good workout and sent me home feeling refreshed. Then an amazing thing happened. My headaches left me. I became less susceptible to colds and the flu. I found that I could work harder, longer, concentrate better. My times in the Word and prayer improved. My only problem had been that I was completely out of shape, and it affected other areas of my life. It's a fact that we humans are wired together spiritually, emotionally, and physically, and when one part suffers it affects the others.

The Apostle Paul has an interesting comment on this, "But I keep under my body, and bring it into subjection: lest that by any means, when I have preached to others, I myself should be a castaway" (1 Cor. 9:27). Notice how he ties in the physical with the spiritual. He kept his body in subjection lest it affect him spiritually and he become a castaway. Amazing!

Balance in intellectual, physical, social, and spiritual growth makes us better persons, more like the Lord Jesus, and more usable in His cause.

Diligence

Is it easier for you to bound out of bed in the morning or roll over for another 30 minutes? Is it easier to mow the lawn tomorrow or today? If you have a lazy streak in you that you just can't seem to shake and it bugs you, you are normal. Note what the psalmist says, "Thou has commanded us to keep Thy precepts diligently" (Ps. 119:4).

The Bible has much to say on the subject of diligence. It has promises to the diligent man as well as to the slothful. The promises are all big ones, some good and some bad. Our job is to decide which set of promises we want to claim. For instance, "How long wilt thou sleep, O sluggard? When wilt thou arise out of thy sleep? Yet a little sleep, a little slumber, a little folding of the hands to sleep; so shall thy poverty come as one that travelleth, and thy want as an armed man" (Prov. 6:9-11). "He also that is slothful in his work is brother to him that is a great waster" (18:9). "The desire of the slothful killeth him; for his hands refuse to labor" (21:25). "He becometh poor that dealeth with a slack hand; but the hand of the diligent maketh rich. He that gathereth in summer is a wise son; but he that sleepeth in harvest is a son that causeth shame" (10:4-5). I'm sure you get the idea.

Now about that lazy streak. If you've got one, cheer up; you've got lots of company. Most of us fight the battle of sloth and laziness. Most of us feel bogged down from time to time with spring fever. We just can't seem to get at things. What's the answer to all that? One answer I've found in my own life is to ask the Lord to give me an overriding purpose in life. Without a purpose life is a drag.

Notice a girl on her wedding day? She's up bright and early, bustling about, chipper, excited, radiant, and she's that way all day. Note the same girl a year later. She drags out of bed, heads for the coffee pot, bleary-eyed, and shuffles through the day. Why? The day holds no purpose, no objective. There is nothing going on that day that she could really throw herself into. She's in a rut. She has no sense of mission or goal.

Suppose one of your purposes is to become a man or woman of God. What can you do? You look at yourself and you see all your weaknesses and lack of knowledge of the Word and shallow prayer life. What will help more than anything is to set some daily short-range goals that are in direct line with that objective. Things such as a time to read the Bible each day, and spending time in prayer. You know that these will help you become more Christlike, and ultimately help you achieve your long-range objective.

Life does not have to be like a rocking chair, in motion but going nowhere. God can show you His purpose and plan for your life. Gear in with that, and life takes on a new flavor that fires your spirit and prompts diligence in your daily life.

Perspective

The jet was flying over the midlands of America on a cloudless day. One of the passengers was watching the ground below with a great degree of fascination. Finally he called the flight attendant over to his seat and asked what all those little squares were down there on the ground. She looked, and patiently explained to him that they were fields of grain. They looked small because the plane was flying at about 36,000 feet. The corn, barley, oats, wheat, and rye all showed up as different shades of green, and the brown squares were fields that had been newly ploughed. After she had gone into great detail with him, she asked if he had any further questions.

His answer was classic. "Yes, I understand all about the wheat fields and corn fields and so on, but what I want to know is: What are all those little squares down there?"

The Christian life can be like that, too. New Christians especially have a tough time learning to gear into their new world. God is very real to the new babe in Christ, but old habit patterns are often hard to break and new activities come slowly. Christians often have a vocabulary all their own. I remember hearing about a young girl who was challenged to have a daily quiet time. She heartily agreed and decided to have it in the afternoon. One day a friend asked her how her quiet time was going.

"Oh, great," she replied. "I get an hour's nap every day from two till three." She was very quiet, but that wasn't exactly what the person meant when she talked about a "quiet time." She meant a time to pray and read the Bible. But from the new Christian's perspective, a quiet time was a time to be quiet. Most people *are* quiet when they are asleep.

I was raised in a Roman Catholic community in southern Iowa. The Catholic Sisters of Mercy across the street from us had statues and candles everywhere. When I became a Christian, and was challenged to have a "family altar," it seemed clear to me what to do. I was about to build an altar in the corner of our living room and set up the kinds of religious articles I had seen across the street. I was stopped in the nick of time. My advisor meant a time to read the Bible and pray as a family, but to someone who viewed it from an entirely different perspective it meant something else.

Older Christians as well can have problems with perspective. I remember what happened to me recently when I visited Corinth, Greece. Frankly I was not looking forward to the trip. The last time I had traveled by car from Athens to Corinth it nearly cost me my life. A truck had been passing another truck on a curve and we met both of them. It was a very close call and the memory was vivid. Nevertheless we decided to go. As we left Athens I saw before us a fine, straight, wide new highway. That put me at ease. The old rough, winding, narrow, and dangerous road had been replaced. So I relaxed and enjoyed the trip.

After spending a few hours walking among the ancient ruins of the old city of Corinth, we started back to Athens. Then it happened. The driver announced, "We're taking the old road back. It is better." I thought to myself, *Better! How could it be better? It is narrow, and dangerous.* I asked him why it was better.

"Oh," he replied, "it goes through the olive groves and is nearer the ocean. You can see flowers and the old houses. It is a prettier way to travel. It is better."

I thought to myself, *That's the way it is in life. It all depends on your perspective.* Here was a man who had traveled this road from his youth. It was like an old friend. He enjoyed seeing the orchards, the sea, and the flowers.

Much of life simply depends on the way you look at it. The Bible says, "In everything give thanks, for this is the will of God in Christ Jesus concerning you" (1 Thes. 5:18). In everything? How in the world can a person do that? By faith—you simply believe the fact that God makes no mistakes, that all things do work together for good to them that love God. When we see things from God's point of view they look different. It all depends on your perspective.

Generosity

We were so far in debt they almost had to pump air down to us and talk to us by radio. My wife had required treatment at the Mayo

Clinic, and my daughter had undergone two eye operations. These added bills, plus another item for $300 that we hadn't planned on, had taxed our faith and salary to the limit. And with three active, growing kids there was the usual round of school clothes, shoes, dental bills, and whatever.

After praying about our debts for some time, my wife and I sat down for a talk. "Virginia," I said, "there's only one thing I know to do. Increase our giving to the Lord's work." We did, and within a matter of weeks we were out of debt. We received some totally unexpected income and once again the statement of Jesus was reinforced in our lives. "Give, and it shall be given unto you; good measure, pressed down, and shaken together, and running over, shall men give unto your bosom. For with the same measure that ye mete withal it shall be measured to you again" (Luke 6:38).

The Bible gives clear, down-to-earth guidelines regarding giving. The Apostle Paul wrote: "But this I say, he which soweth bountifully shall reap also bountifully. Every man according as he purposeth in his heart, so let him give; not grudgingly, or of necessity, for God loveth a cheerful giver" (2 Cor. 9:6-7). The first principle he lays down is that we should give bountifully, because we reap in proportion to what we sow.

There are times, however, when to give generously would be hard and would call for sacrifice. In that light, one Old Testament story has been a challenge to me. David wanted to buy the threshing floor of Araunah for use as a place of sacrifice to the Lord. When Araunah learned of King David's desire, he offered it to the king free of charge. (See 2 Sam. 24:22.)

David's answer to Araunah is classic: "Nay, but I will surely buy it of thee at a price. Neither will I offer burnt offerings unto the Lord my God of that which doth cost me nothing" (24:24). As the offering plate passes by on Sunday morning, do we toss into the plate that which really requires no sacrifice at all, that which costs us nothing?

The second principle the apostle mentions is that we should give purposefully, deliberately, with a plan. We should think through our financial situation and determine where we want to begin in our giving to the Lord. Like any other grace, this one must develop and mature as we develop and mature in our faith and walk with God. A good place to start, of course, is with the tithe, which means one-tenth. Using that as a base, let the Lord broaden and increase it as He will. As our faith grows we can increase our giving. A strong giving program cannot be built on a weak foundation of faith. And we should determine before the Lord where our giving will be directed. Our local church, missions, special projects or overseas areas where famine or earthquake or floods call for emergency help. Deliberate, purposeful giving is a must.

The third principle is to give freely, expecting nothing in return. God gave freely out of His love for us (see John 3:16). To follow His example in any area of life is sure to be a blessing, and giving is no exception. Of course, to give because we feel we must, to give grudgingly, to give out of necessity is of little value. A cheerful heart must accompany money to speed it on its way under the blessing of God.

In the Old Testament the people of God were required to give one-tenth of their income. This was given to maintain a rather static society of religious worship. Then Jesus came and let everybody know that the ingrown, limited religious activities with which the Jews had become so familiar was no longer the norm. From now on it was world conquest. Men were challenged to take the message of salvation to the ends of the earth and preach it to every person. Immediately the work of God moved into an expanding, global thrust. The message was to be planted in the uttermost parts of the earth.

If it took 10 percent to maintain the static society of the nation Israel, what will it take to keep the momentum of a global mission strong and flourishing? Ten percent? Yes, and more! That's why each of us must keep in close fellowship with the Lord Himself in order that He might lead us in our giving, that our giving might reflect His great gift to us, "For ye know the grace of our Lord Jesus Christ, that, though He was rich, yet for your sakes He became poor, that ye through His poverty might be rich" (2 Cor. 8:9).

Growth in Grace

The Christian life is all by grace from first to last. Good works are the fruit of the life of the Lord within the Christian as he grows in grace and in the knowledge of Christ. "For by grace are ye saved through faith; and that not of yourselves, it is the gift of God, not of works, lest any man should boast. For we are His workmanship, created in Christ Jesus unto good works, which God hath before ordained that we should walk in them" (Eph. 2:8-10).

Christian living is to be clean and pure, and that is possible only when God has daily control of our lives. Therefore we must rely on Him and Him alone, not on our self-efforts toward victory over sin, peace of heart, or concern for the lost.

The problem arises when we look at ourselves and see how far short we fall of God's Word. But the key issue is not what we are, but what we are becoming. Is my life headed in the right direction? Is my heart open to the challenge, instruction, reproof, and correction of the Holy Spirit as He speaks to me from the Scriptures?

It is not the degree of progress but our attitudes that are decisive. Growth in love and holiness is neither mechanical nor magical. It is accomplished by God in daily fellowship with Him, in which we give ourselves to Him in hope, faith, and obedience. It is not just a negative thing, the mere separation from sin, but a positive, progressive thing where our lives grow in capacity and character into the stature of the fullness of Christ (see Eph. 4:13).

Does all of this cause you to throw up your hands in despair? Good! That's the first step. You are well on your way to realizing first-hand, the truth of Jesus' statement, "I am the vine, ye are the branches. He that abideth in Me, and I in him, the same bringeth forth much fruit; for without Me ye can do nothing" (John 15:5). All the resources of the Christian life are in Christ alone. You are a branch of the vine and a branch cannot bear fruit by any effort of its own. Fruit in your life is produced by the life of Christ in you and all the things you long for: peace, growth, holiness, good works —all are part of that fruit. That's how a disciple lives under the Lordship of Christ.

Prologue to Chapter 7

The life of a disciple who is maturing in the faith is not his own. He can no longer do as he pleases, go where he pleases, spend his money as he pleases, or act the way he pleases. Christ is becoming Lord of his life and there are certain demands made on his time and energy.

A disciple is called on to share his faith with others, give his money to further the world mission of Christ, and be available to the Spirit of God to overflow his life with good works.

In spite of your heavy schedule, your responsibilities to your home, family, and others, and the constant demands on your time, I want to encourage you to a life of productive service for Christ. This chapter emphasizes the importance of doing the things that are consonant with your being a child of your heavenly Father and a disciple of Christ.

7

What a Disciple Does

Disciples of Christ live among people for whom life has become a drag—so blah, so meaningless, so colorless! That is why it is so important for Christians to live the life of joy and purpose before them. People you'd never expect find life really dull. Some ask the question, "Is there life after birth?"

A Life That Has Purpose and Meaning

A young man I know was on an athletic scholarship at a large university. He now has his Ph.D., has more money than he needs, and all that money will buy, yet he's miserable. He called me on the phone a while back and said, "You know, LeRoy, I'm no better off than a horse. I go to work, I eat, I sleep, but there's no color in my life. It's all a dull gray." Here he was, a young man on his way to California for a costly vacation, driving a new sportscar, with a suitcase full of new and expensive clothes, who found life a living death.

A campus newspaper ran a contest to see who could write a definition of life. Three that won honorable mention were: Life is a bad joke that's not funny / Life is a disease for which there is no cure / Life is a jail sentence you get for being born. A doctor said, "One-third of my patients are suffering from the senselessness of their lives." I heard a man say he had tried Ovaltine, tiger milk, Di-Gel, Geritol, yogurt, wheat germ, Crest, and Ban, and *still* there was something missing.

It does seem strange to some that things and temporal pleasures don't really satisfy. The reason is that we're told over and over again that they will. The television reminds us every 10 minutes or so that this or that product is just what we need. Travel agencies show us pictures of paradise and encourage us to leave home and find it all out there somewhere.

A person can struggle to make it to the top of the financial heap and be bitterly disappointed. My friend who lives at the pinnacle of financial success says when you make it to the top you find broken marriages, high blood pressure, heart attacks, ulcers, alcoholism, drugs, and suicide. But most people don't believe that, so they keep on climbing. It's something like the old Laurel and Hardy movie in which one of them was digging a hole and the other was filling it up. They were working their fingers to the bone and getting nowhere. Like the little squirrel on the circular treadmill, they are running at top speed and not really moving. Life doesn't have to be all that complicated.

There's an answer, of course. The problem is that people don't realize that man is basically a spiritual being. God breathed into man the breath of life and man became a living soul. Man is more than an animal. He's made in the likeness of God, and his deepest needs cannot be fulfilled by material things. The Bible says Jesus increased in wisdom and stature and in favor with God and man (Luke 2:52). The verse shows the four areas of personal development: Intellectual, physical, spiritual, and social. Leave out the spiritual part and you've left out real life. Jesus said, "I am come that they might have life, and that they might have it more abundantly" (John 10:10).

A young graduate student at the University of Maryland told me, "Before I came to Christ, my life was like a black and white photograph, but now it's like a three-dimensional Kodachrome— full of color and depth." He had been born anew—being born again from above is what brought this beautiful change.

Jesus said, "I am the way, the truth, and the life" (John 14:6). He didn't say, "I will teach you about life." He said, "I *am* the life." There is life after birth, and it is found in the person of the Lord Jesus Christ. And day after day, He holds out His hand to offer it to the world. And He does it through you.

The Life That Is Too Good to Be True
Your life as a disciple of Christ is going to be closely watched

by many unbelievers, because the Gospel message sounds to them just too good to be true.

Most people live in constant fear of death. The Christian, who has the assurance of salvation, does not. "These things have I written unto you that believe on the name of the Son of God; that ye may know that ye have eternal life, and that ye may believe on the name of the Son of God" (1 John 5:13).

Most people fear economic problems. The Christian does not. He has the assurance of provision of his daily needs. "But my God shall supply all your need according to His riches in glory by Christ Jesus" (Phil. 4:19).

Most people who pray wonder if they are being heard. The Christian knows God as the One who hears and answers prayer. God says, "Call unto Me, and I will answer thee, and show thee great and mighty things, which thou knowest not" (Jer. 33:3).

Most people are concerned about the future. The Christian is not. "Trust in the Lord with all thine heart, and lean not unto thine own understanding. In all thy ways acknowledge Him, and He shall direct thy paths" (Prov. 3:5-6).

This often sounds too good to be true—but it is *true*.

I was lecturing to a class in a university in Germany. After a 30-minute presentation of the Gospel of Christ, a group of a dozen or so students came to the front of the classroom to talk. They said, "Mr. Eims, you are *utopian*. Nothing could be that good. What you say is just too good to be true." We went from there to the student union and had lunch together and discussed the matter for a couple of hours. Those Germans were a tough bunch to convince, but I think we made a little progress so that a few of them were seriously considering the claims of Christ.

I encountered the same problem at the University of Idaho. After a presentation of the Gospel, I opened up the meeting to questions from the audience. A young man stood up in the back of the room and said, "I've been listening to all of this and I think you're lying. Nothing could be as good as you make it out to be."

Immediately a girl in the center of the room stood up. She was a large girl—not overweight, but big bones and muscles. It turned out that she was a lady shot-putter. She was dressed in a leather jacket and she appeared quite formidable. She raised her voice and said, "Buddy, this man is not lying. And this is *not* too good to be true. A few months ago I received Jesus Christ into my life and He has done for me exactly what this man said tonight." The young man sat down. He had appeared quite belligerent at first, but now he was as quiet as a lamb. I don't think he wanted to tangle with the lady shot-putter. Maybe he thought she was going to shot the put at him—or put the shot, or however you say that. In any event, her testimony seemed to be just what was needed at the time.

Too good to be true? I'm sure that's how it appears from a human standpoint. But we must never forget or minimize the grace and mercy of God. By His own choice, God has decided to extend His mercy to us. The mercy of God is the special act of God whereby He keeps from us that which we rightfully deserve because of our sins.

The psalmist repeats "For His mercy endureth forever" 26 times in Psalm 136. By way of contrast, the grace of God is the special act of God whereby He showers on us that to which we have no right—His unmerited favor. The Bible says, "Let us therefore come boldly unto the throne of grace, that we may obtain mercy, and find grace to help in time of need" (Heb. 4:16). The Scriptures glow with the precious promises of God.

The very fact that the life Jesus offers appears too good to be true testifies to its divine origin. Certainly no *man* could have devised such a life. And no man could live such a life apart from the power of God. There's the secret. A daily walk with our Maker, and the life that appears just too good to be true will be ours.

A Visual Aid

A friend of mine is a manager of one of the largest and most prestigious hotels in the Middle East. His job is very demanding; the hotel is usually full; it has a standard of excellence to maintain; VIPs from the four corners of the earth stay there when they are in that part of the world, and of course, everybody expects to be treated like he's the only person in the hotel. Phones are ringing constantly in his office, secretaries and assistants demanding decisions. Everyone who knows him is amazed that he has such a capacity to get so much done. But that's not nearly as amazing as the fact that in the midst of it all, he always has a smile. He remains calm and stable. John Abbushibble of the Phoenicia Hotel in Beirut, Lebanon has learned a secret.

John has a personal campaign on to help his friends and associates experience the wonderful gift of life that he has received from God. Some years ago he became a Christian. Now he smiles and tells his friends, "You don't know what you are missing." His words have the ring of reality. I met with some of his friends at a businessmen's luncheon, and they were all impressed by his life.

That's often the missing link in the Christian enterprise. When the non-Christian drives by the church on Sunday morning on his way to the golf course or to the beach, and hears the congregation singing the hymns of the faith, he thinks to himself, *Well, every man to his own kick. If that's what they enjoy, more power to them.* He prefers golf or the sun and the surf and the sand. If that is all he sees of Christianity he is unimpressed. But when he sees a person with that something extra that he admires, he is often led to ask, "What makes you that way? How are you able to keep calm when the situation calls for panic? How can you face the future with such quiet assurance when the headlines point to disaster and constant trouble?"

I'm sure that's why God has said in His Word, "And I sought for a man among them" (Ezek. 22:30). Notice the words "among them." This is the age-old search of God, a search that's as new as our unborn sons and as old as the dawn of man.

Why is it that Christians do not always have that kind of life in the marketplace of the world? Often it is because they have been taught to look at Christianity as a set of facts to believe or a creed to embrace. But the kingdom of God is not in word but in power. There is more to it than just permitting oneself to be jammed into somebody's theological mold. True Christianity experiences the controlling power of God in daily life, as the Lord Jesus Christ lives His life through the believer. Creedal Christians are cradle Christians. Maturity is manifested when the Word of God becomes reality on the job, in the home, at school, or at play.

People need a visual aid to the kingdom of God. Visual aids are constantly used today to communicate the message. In the sales meeting or the staff meeting or the Sunday School class, you will find the chalkboard or the overhead projector or the slide presentation. All well and good. The best visual aid to graphically portray the kingdom of God is a life that is lived in fellowship with Jesus Christ. That's something the non-Christian can see. It has a powerful effect on him. He can't deny it. It's there.

Telling What We Know

Jesus said, "Ye shall be witnesses unto Me" (Acts 1:8). You and I have a personal experience of Jesus Christ in our lives. We have tested His teachings and found them to be true. We can speak with conviction and authority because we are telling what we know. Our testimony is not hearsay but history. "That which we have seen and heard declare we unto you, that ye also may have fellowship with us; and truly our fellowship is with the Father, and with His Son Jesus Christ" (1 John 1:3).

Every child of God is a member of a great witnessing brotherhood. God has graciously gifted certain divinely appointed men to teach and train us to do our job better, but witnessing is everybody's job. The Bible says, "He gave some apostles, and some prophets, and some evangelists, and some pastors and teachers, for the perfecting of the saints, for the work of the ministry, for the edifying of the body of Christ" (Eph. 4:11-12).

To be an effective witness for Christ we must be in intimate fellowship with Him. Last fall my family enjoyed tomatoes, potatoes, peas, and beans from our garden. I especially liked the squash. As these vines began to mature, they spread in every direction. One of the branches crawled across the path that leads down into the creek that runs through our backyard. One day someone stepped on that branch and severed it from the vine. It stopped growing and withered away. It bore no fruit. So it is in our lives as Christians. We must maintain a close fellowship with the Lord Jesus if we would have our lives bear fruit. His statement is clear. "Without Me ye can do nothing" (John 15:15). Fellowship with the Lord Jesus is not optional.

Second, to be effective we must pray. Pray specifically by name for those who need the Saviour. Ask God to prepare the hearts of people for your witness. The Bible says to be persistent in prayer. Pray that God will give you many opportunities to share His message. Make a list of people who need the Saviour and pray that God will prepare the soil of their hearts for the seed of His Word.

Third, share God's Word. Note these examples. "Then Philip opened his mouth, and began at the same Scripture, and preached unto him Jesus" (Acts 8:35). "And Paul, as his manner was, went in unto them, and three Sabbath days reasoned with them out of the Scriptures" (17:2). So as we pray and plant the seed of the Word of God, the Holy Spirit takes that Word and germinates it and a new life results. Jesus said, "Behold, there went out a sower to sow. . . . The sower soweth the Word" (Mark 4:3, 14). Why? Because we are born again, not of corruptible seed, but of incorruptible, by the Word of God. The Gospel of Jesus Christ is not primarily persuasive, but creative. It creates new life. "For I am not ashamed of the Gospel of Christ, for it is the power of God unto salvation to every one that believeth, to the Jew first, and also to the Greek" (Rom. 1:16).

Share the Word of God so that people understand clearly how to receive Christ into their lives. Jesus said, "But he that received seed into the good ground is he that heareth the Word, and understandeth it, which also beareth fruit, and bringeth forth, some an hundredfold, some sixty, and some thirty" (Matt. 13:23).

Many fine booklets can help you make the Gospel clear. These may be purchased from your local Christian bookstore or ordered directly from the publishers.*

The Great Commission

They had seen Him captured and condemned by the Jewish authorities. They had seen Him beaten and judged by the power of Rome. They had seen Him hang helpless on a cross. They had seen Him carried lifeless to a tomb. But there He stood now, victor over death. Back from the grave. His words carried an authority and strength that set these men on the course they would follow for the rest of their lives. These words are recorded five times in the New Testament. "Jesus came and spoke unto them, saying, 'All power is given unto Me in heaven and in earth. Go ye therefore, and teach all nations, baptizing them in the name of the Father, and of the Son, and of the Holy Ghost, teaching

---

* *Do you Know the Steps to Peace with God?* The Billy Graham Evangelistic Association, Box 779, Minneapolis, Minn. 55440; *Have You Heard of the Four Spiritual Laws?* Campus Crusade for Christ International, Arrowhead Springs, San Bernardino, Calif. 92404; and *The Bridge to Life,* The Navigators, P.O. Box 1659, Colorado Springs, Colo. 80901.

them to observe all things whatsoever I have commanded you; and, lo, I am with you alway, even unto the end of the world' " (Matt. 28:18-20). Here Jesus told His followers to teach, or make disciples, of all nations. You'll notice in verse 16 that the charge was given to the eleven disciples. The reason the command to make disciples was given to men who were disciples was because to make disciples you must be a disciple. It takes one to make one.

In Mark's account we learn something more of the scope of the enterprise—to every creature, "Go ye into all the world, and preach the Gospel to every creature" (Mark 16:15). The message of the Gospel was to be taken to every person.

The record in Luke gives instructions as to how to go about it. "Then opened He their understanding, that they might understand the Scriptures, and said unto them, 'Thus it is written, and thus it behoved Christ to suffer, and to rise from the dead the third day; and that repentance and remission of sins should be preached in His name among all nations, beginning at Jerusalem' " (Luke 24:45-57). They were to preach repentance and remission of sins through Jesus Christ. They were to begin at Jerusalem. The target was all nations. He taught them truths that would clarify and deepen their understanding of the Scriptures: the Gospel, the suffering, death, burial, and resurrection of Christ and the world mission. These great doctrines are the keys to a clear grasp of the rest of Scripture. When we clearly understand the Gospel and understand our personal involvement in the Great Commission, the rest of Scripture takes on new meaning and importance.

John tells us something of the cost involved. "The same day at evening, being the first day of the week, when the doors were shut where the disciples were assembled for fear of the Jews, came Jesus and stood in the midst, and saith unto them, 'Peace be unto you.' And when He had so said, He showed unto them His hands and His side. Then were the disciples glad, when they saw the Lord. Then said Jesus to them again, 'Peace be unto you; as My Father hath sent Me, even so send I you' " (John 20:19-21). As He showed them His hands and His side, He said, "As My Father hath sent Me, even so send I you." His hands were ripped open from being thrust through with nails. His side carried the mark of the spear. They got the message. It was not going to be an easy task. The servant was no greater than his Lord. They could expect persecution, opposition, and trials.

In the Book of Acts we have His last words: " 'But ye shall receive power, after that the Holy Ghost is come upon you; and ye shall be witnesses unto me both in Jerusalem, and in all Judea, and in Samaria, and unto the uttermost part of the earth.' And when He had spoken these things, while they beheld, He was taken up, and a cloud received Him out of their sight" (Acts 1:8-9). Here the strategy of the mission is laid out. Jerusalem, Judea, Samaria, and then to the far corners of the earth. As we study the Book of Acts, we can see how this was followed to the letter. First Jerusalem and Judea heard the message. Then Philip carried the Gospel to Samaria. And finally the Apostle Peter was used of God to open the door to the Gentiles as Cornelius, the Roman centurion, received the message (see Acts 10).

After Jesus had given the commission for the final time, He returned to heaven. Two things are important to note at this point. One, these were His final words. The last words of a commander supercede all other commands. They are the instructions we follow. Secondly, He was taken up while they beheld. He did it in full view. They watched Him. Later, when denial was demanded, they had the bedrock assurance that He was alive forevermore. They had seen Him taken up.

John tells us, "In Him was life; and the life was the light of men" (John 1:4). Life and light were embodied in Jesus. He said, "The thief cometh not but to steal, and to kill, and to destroy; I come that they might have life" (10:10). He also said, "I am the light of the world; he that followeth Me shall not walk in darkness, but shall have the light of life" (8:12). The writer of Hebrews tells us that Jesus came to deliver us from the bondage of the fear of death. "And deliver them who, through fear of death, were all their lifetime subject to bondage" (Heb. 2:15). Paul wrote, "Who hath delivered us from the power of darkness, and hath translated us into the kingdom of His dear Son" (Col. 1:13).

You and I are given the same privilege. As disciples of Jesus, the Great Commission is our commission. The same conditions prevail and the same urgency is there. Millions are lost in the dark, and dying without Christ. The message is clear. The mandate is clear—to live our lives and govern our affairs in the light of the Great Commission. The Old Testament Scriptures predict Christ's Great Commission. Time and time again they record the grand theme of making God's name known in all the world. When God dried up the waters of the Jordan while the people of God crossed into the Promised Land, one of the expected results of this miracle was "that all the people of the earth might know the hand of the Lord, that it is mighty" (Josh. 4:24).

One of the most famous confrontations in the entire Bible was between David and Goliath. In his challenge to Goliath, David cried out what was on his heart: "That all the earth may know that there is a God in Israel" (1 Sam. 17:46). This theme carried over in his psalm as well: "Blessed be the Lord God, the God of Israel, who only doeth wondrous things. And blessed be His glorious name forever; and let the whole earth be filled with His glory" (Ps. 72:18-19).

Some years later Solomon, his son, built the great temple in Jerusalem. In his prayer of dedication he said, "Hear Thou in heaven, Thy dwelling place, and do according to all that the stranger calleth to Thee for, that all people of the earth may know Thy name, to fear Thee, as do Thy people Israel; and that they may know that this house, which I have builded, is called by Thy name" (1 Kings 8:43). After he had finished his prayer, he pronounced a blessing upon the people. Concluding his God-inspired blessing on the people, he said, "That all the people of the earth may know that the Lord is God, and that there is none else" (8:60).

Years later King Hezekiah was attacked by the enemies of God and received a blasphemous letter which Sennacherib sent to reproach the living God. Hezekiah turned to the Lord in prayer. "Now therefore, O Lord our God, I beseech Thee, save Thou us out of his hand, that all the kingdoms of the earth may know that Thou art the Lord God, even Thou only" (2 Kings 19:19).

These illustrations point out that it has always been God's intent that His name should be known throughout all the earth. With that fact as a background, it is obvious that the Son of God would commission men to carry His message to the ends of the earth. In the Old Testament, God's power was revealed as giants fell, battles raged, a temple was built, and water stood up in a heap, that God's name might be spread throughout the whole earth. Note Paul's testimony: "I am not ashamed of the Gospel of Christ; for it is the power of God unto salvation to everyone that believeth; to the Jew first, and also to the Greek" (Rom. 1:16). Now God's power is unleashed as a message is given.

Through it all, one constant remains: dedicated people—David the shepherd boy, Joshua the soldier, Solomon and Hezekiah the kings. In the New Testament we see Peter the fisherman, Luke the physician, Matthew the tax collector, and by the grace of God, you and me. The Great Commission is our commission.

As we hear the words of Christ, we ask ourselves if it is really possible to get a message to the whole world. Consider for a moment the Roman plan: "It came to pass, in those days, that there went out a decree from Caesar Augustus, that all the world should be taxed" (Luke 2:1). Did Caesar get the job done? Did everyone hear and respond? As we read the subsequent account it becomes evident that the answer is yes. Even those living in the remote Judean hills got the word.

In light of that, consider God's plan: "I will raise Me up a faithful priest, who shall do according to that which is in Mine heart and in My mind; and I will build him a sure house, and he shall walk before Mine anointed forever" (1 Sam. 2:35). God had something on His heart and mind. The same is true today. God has the world on His heart.

The Apostle Paul, under divine inspiration, reveals God's basic strategy to accomplish His grand design and his own involvement in it. "Whom we preach, warning every man, and teaching every man in all wisdom, that we may present every man perfect in Christ Jesus. Whereunto I also labor, striving according to His working, which worketh in me mightily" (Col. 1:28-29). This is a simple plan: Share the Gospel and train those who respond to repeat the process. Paul worked at that all the time with all the strength God gave him.

What a beautiful, exciting idea. All of us can do that. There is room for everyone. God's plan for the world does not require a superstar. Each of us can be involved and have a part. The only requirement is that we be disciples of Christ, because the commission is to make disciples and it takes one to make one. God does not use a lie to teach the truth. He does not use a person with a weak and anemic run-down-at-the-heels prayer life to help a young believer learn to have power in prayer. He does not use a person with a cold, indifferent attitude toward the Bible to help someone else become strong in the Word.

If we are to make disciples, we must be disciples. God will take our lives and use us to help fulfill the highest calling on earth: We'll be personally involved in the commission of Christ to make Him known in all the world.

The Treasure in the Cave

A certain cave in the Holy Land looks just like scores of other caves in the area. But this is the one everybody comes to see. And no wonder. The treasure that was found in it made headlines around the world. Yet the shepherd who found it didn't know it was worth anything.

The shepherd, realizing that one of his goats was missing, went to search the countryside. When he saw the cave he wondered if his goat had fallen in, so he tossed a rock down into it to see if he could cause any movement. All he heard was the sound of pottery breaking. Coins from the distant past? Was there a treasure in the cave? Silver or gold? It was too dark to enter so the shepherd decided to wait till morning.

At the crack of dawn he went up to the cave, lowered himself in and found some earthen pots. To his disgust and disappointment they contained nothing but brittle old scrolls. He took one and used it to start a fire. He decided to take along a few with him. Possibly they might be worth something. When he returned to Bethlehem he sold them for $10. The man who purchased them tried to sell them to a university in the Middle East. No one would take them. So he took them to New York and found some people who understood their worth. The man who bought them from the shepherd for $10 sold them for $750,000. From that the world learned of the discovery of the Dead Sea Scrolls.

That which at first appeared worthless is now housed in the Shrine of the Book in Jerusalem. Thousands of people come to see the ancient and valuable treasure which was discovered in an earthen vessel by a simple shepherd, who had no idea of what he had found.

As I stood by the cave, and later in the Shrine of the Book, looking at the scrolls, I was reminded of the Scripture, "But we have this treasure in earthen vessels, that the excellency of the power may be of God, and not of us" (2 Cor. 4:7). Paul speaks of two treasures here. One, the glorious Gospel of Christ, the message that has delivered us from the power of darkness and has translated us into the kingdom of His dear Son.

We were allowed of God to be put in trust with the Gospel. That which God used to bring us to Himself, He has placed in our trust to share with others. We must not fail in this trust. Our friends and neighbors must hear the glorious message that Jesus Christ has come to bring life and immortality to light through the Gospel.

The second treasure that Paul speaks of is the glory of God. "For God, who commanded the light to shine out of darkness, hath shined in our hearts, to give the light of the knowledge of the glory of God in the face of Jesus Christ" (2 Cor. 4:6). What a warm, intimate experience with the living God as He reveals His glory in Christ! A treasure in earthen vessels!

We cannot hoard this treasure—it was given to share. There are countless Christians living in oppressive societies who would give anything to have the high privilege of freely sharing their faith. As you know, in some countries of the world, it is against the law to witness. People have been beaten, tortured, imprisoned, and killed for sharing this treasure with a friend.

Today God calls on each of us to realize that we have the eternal riches of Christ that the Holy Spirit can take and meet the spiritual hunger and moral bankruptcy of the world.

Prologue to Chapter 8

Almost everything we do as disciples could affect how others view the new life offered them in Jesus Christ. Besides this silent witness which we bear to the Gospel, there are specific times when we should be active and open in our testimony to others.

We are all different, our personalities and backgrounds are different, and the people to whom we bear testimony are different. So, each testimony we give and each attempt to witness bears some uniqueness as well. While this is true, there are certain common problems faced in trying to witness for Christ which you would do well to consider at this point in your growing experience. This chapter is going to talk about some of the "How-to" of witnessing for Christ, to give you some practical help as you begin.

8

How to Be an Effective
Witness for Christ

Witnessing is the overflow of the life of Christ within us. Too often we think that if we master a method of sharing the Gospel, or learn to use this tool, or that one, God will use our lives to bring others to Himself.

It is important to be able to share the Gospel message clearly. The Bible says, "He that received seed into the good ground is he that heareth the Word, and understandeth it" (Matt. 13:23). But the real secret of a fruitful life is found in Jesus' words: "I am the vine, ye are the branches. He that abideth in Me, and I in him, the same bringeth forth much fruit, for without Me ye can do nothing" (John 15:5). To abide in Christ means to have intimate, personal, two-way communication with Him as He speaks to us through the Word, and we speak to Him in prayer.

As we meet with the Lord we can ask Him to lead us to those who have hungry hearts. Thousands of people are sin-sick, fed up with life, bored stiff, knowing there is something more in life, knowing their lives are not complete. They have no idea which way to turn. So often they seek in strange and dangerous places, false cults, the occult, and guidance from the stars. Some turn to narcotics and alcohol, trying to find that which will complete their lives. When they hear the message of Christ, it has the ring of truth. But often they have to wait till someone tells them the answers which can really satisfy.

The people of God are often like a group standing in the corner of a field that is ripe and ready to be harvested. But they are not heading into the field, sleeves rolled up, ready to go to work. Rather, they are involved in other things. One group is haggling. While the crop rots and falls to the ground they are arguing with each other. Because they can't seem to get along, the crop is left unattended.

In another corner another group is busy preparing to harvest. But the problem is that they have been preparing for years. Someone had come along and told them that they had to be polished theologians before they could work in the harvest. They had to know soteriology, eschatology, ecclesiology, Hebrew, Greek, psychology, ancient literature, and science. They feel unqualified. But when you take a closer look you can see that they already have more education than they need to bring in the dying harvest. And so on around the field, you find people doing everything *but* harvesting.

Sharing Your New Life in Christ

When you have opportunity to witness for Christ, remember that a word of personal testimony packs a wallop. I was at Harvard University having lunch with three students. My friend was in law school there, and had invited two of his friends, one a new Christian and one a non-Christian. The fellow who was not a Christian and I got into a philosophical discussion about God, the universe, and religion.

I saw I was getting nowhere with him, and was wondering what to do when the new Christian said, "Well, I don't know about all that, but I do know this. A few weeks ago I invited Jesus into my heart, and He forgave all my sins and gave me a new life." The student I had been talking to stopped eating and looked up in amazement.

"He did?" he asked.

"Yes! I invited Him into my heart and He came in and it's wonderful!"

The philosophical discussion was forgotten. I was forgotten. He turned to the young Christian and began a serious discussion as to how *he* could find this new life. Frankly, I was ashamed of myself. I should have known better. Here was a young Christian, bursting with his new life in Christ, sharing a few verses he had memorized, giving his testimony, the life of Christ overflowing into the heart and life of another.

We have an excellent example of sharing our faith in the way that Paul gave his testimony (see Acts 22; 26). He told what his life was like before Christ came in; then he told how he met the Lord, and then related some of the new changes that had taken place since he met the Lord.

You can always tell others what the Lord has done for you. Let His life overflow into the life of another. Ask the Lord for opportunities to share simply and clearly the facts about your life in Christ. You'll be amazed at the number of people who will find your testimony interesting and meaningful. God will use it to point the way to new life in Christ.*

Giving Your Testimony
No one can deny history. The facts that the Wright Brothers flew their airplane at Kitty Hawk, or that George Washington was the first president of the United States, or that my daughter Becky was born on January 5, 1952, are undeniable. These things are a part of the record. They do not stir up argument. When you recite history to a person you are not dealing with philosophical theory or speculation. Facts are facts, and that's that. For this reason, each Christian has a remarkably powerful story to tell that cannot be denied, the story of his personal experience and relationship with God.

When the Apostle Paul gave his testimony (see Acts 22; 26), you will notice that though his story was very personal, full of "I," "me," and "my," which of course, it had to be, he kept Christ central. Though he told essentially the same story both times, he adapted it to the different people to whom he was speaking that it would be clearly understood.

To do your best when you speak of Christ, you should look at the greatest example of effective communication who ever lived, the Lord Jesus Christ Himself. "Never man spake like this Man" (John 7:46). No one before or since. What did He do that was different? Three Scriptures give insight into this matter. The first is: "They were astonished at His doctrine for He taught them as one that had authority, and not as the scribes" (Mark 1:22). The scribes were like schoolboys reciting lessons, but Jesus spoke as one sent from God. He spoke with the power of personal convic-

---

*I develop this theme in depth in *Winning Ways*. This book may be purchased from your local Christian bookstore, or ordered directly from Victor Books, P.O. Box 1825, Wheaton, Ill. 60187 (Cat. No. 6-2707).

tion. A quiet, humble statement of actual experience captures the attention of your hearers.

The second Scripture is: "All bare Him witness, and wondered at the gracious words which proceeded out of His mouth" (Luke 4:22). Jesus spoke in a gracious manner. He was not overbearing and offensive. The Apostle Paul wrote to the Ephesians about "speaking the truth in love" (Eph. 4:15). Truth spoken in love is a powerful instrument in the hand of the Holy Spirit because "love never fails" (1 Cor. 13:8, AMP).

The third Scripture is: "They were astonished at His doctrine, for His Word was with power" (Luke 4:32). This was the power that came from a desire to bring glory to His Father in heaven, and to do His will. He said, "I can of Mine own self do nothing. As I hear, I judge, and My judgment is just, because I seek not Mine own will, but the will of the Father which hath sent Me. If I bear witness of Myself, My witness is not true" (John 5:30-31). His life gave His words power. Paul speaks of this. "For our Gospel came not unto you in word only, but also in power, and in the Holy Ghost, and in much assurance, as ye know what manner of men we were among you for your sake" (1 Thes. 1:5). In Christ we find the authority of personal experience and conviction spoken in a gracious and loving way with the power of humility and the desire to bring glory to God.

Use the Scripture to document the truth of your words. Your personal experience, coupled with a meaningful verse or two from the Bible, will pack a wallop. The Holy Spirit will use it to do His work in the heart to convict of sin, righteousness, and judgment. Make the story of your encounter with Christ so clear that another person hearing your testimony will know how to receive the Lord.

Being an Ambassador for Christ

An ambassador needs three things to do his job well: preparation, credentials, and instructions. An ambassador is an important person in that he represents his king or his government to a foreign country. The Apostle Paul says that we are ambassadors for Christ (2 Cor. 5:20). You and I have the blessed and awesome responsibility of representing the Lord Jesus Christ, the King of kings and Lord of lords, to the people of the earth to whom He has sent us.

Imagine what would happen if an American ambassador was asked what his country's policy was on a particular matter, and the ambassador flushed with embarrassment and began to shuffle through his briefcase saying that he knew the answer was in there somewhere, but he just couldn't find it. Have you ever seen an ambassador of Christ do that? I have. He fumbles through His Bible, uncertain of the location of the verse he needs, unfamiliar with the source of information. He has the only source of information that tells of eternal matters, yet he doesn't know his Bible. He is unskillful in the Word of Righteousness.

A friend of mine tells of an incident when he was a new student at Moody Bible Institute. He was assigned to a Gospel team preaching the Gospel on the streets. After a song or two, a word of testimony, and a Gospel message, the group fanned out among the crowd and spoke with them individually. Norm spoke to a man sitting against a building and asked him if he wanted to receive Christ into his life. The man said yes.

Norm was amazed. It was his first time out and he hadn't expected that sort of response. Norm looked at his Bible, then thumbed from Genesis to Revelation and found nothing familiar. He thought maybe if he went from front to back something familiar would show up, so he went from Revelation to Genesis, and he still found nothing that he recognized. So he looked at the man, blurted out, "May God bless you," and went away, angry and frustrated with himself.

Norm determined that day that he would learn his Bible thoroughly, and he did. Today if you talked to this man you would find a life saturated with the Scriptures.

As ambassadors of Christ, we must know our message. We must be able to present the Gospel clearly and simply. We must be able to share the message of salvation so that people can make an intelligent decision to receive Christ.

Look again at the three requisites of good ambassadors of Christ. We certainly have credentials. We go in the name of the Father, the Son, and the Holy Spirit. We are ambassadors of Christ. We certainly have instructions. "Go ye into all the world, and preach the Gospel to every creature" (Mark 16:15). Go and make disciples among all nations. Preparation, the third requirement, is what many of us are lacking. Here is where we must covenant with God to learn His Word, to lay up His Word in our hearts—to memorize the Scriptures—in order that we may have an answer for every man that asks us the reason of the hope that is in us (see 1 Peter 3:15).*

Presenting the Gospel

Paul said, "I am not ashamed of the Gospel of Christ, for it is the power of God unto salvation to everyone that believeth, to the Jew first, and also to the Greek" (Rom. 1:16). From the same Greek word for *power* used here, we get the English word "dynamo" and "dynamite." One way of seeing the power of God unleashed on the world is to unleash the Gospel.

The word *gospel* means "good news." When you read the daily paper you begin to realize that there is very little good news around. To a world burdened with bad news, God has given us the Gospel to proclaim. A message of good news that is dynamite, but in a constructive, not a destructive sense. The Gospel is beautifully summarized by Paul: "I delivered unto you first of all that which I also received, how that Christ died for our sins according to the Scriptures, and that He was buried, and that He rose again the third day according to the Scriptures" (1 Cor. 15:3-4).

Several verses are important to remember when witnessing that will help you make the message clear.

1. *Romans 3:23:* "For all have sinned and come short of the glory of God." It points out the simple truth that nobody's perfect. We're all in the same boat. Nobody has lived up to his own standards of what he knows he should be, let alone lived up to God's standards. We've all sinned, we've all come short.

2. *Romans 6:23:* "For the wages of sin is death, but the gift of God is eternal life through Jesus Christ our Lord." I heard a minister say that in every case but two in the New Testament where the word *death* was used, it meant separation. That makes sense. Sin always separates. A husband sins against his wife, and there's a separation. Not always in the legal sense, but it's there. One man steals all the negotiable stocks and bonds from his business partner and there's a separation. There's not the feeling of warmth and companionship there was before. Sin always separates.

---

*The Navigators have published a Scripture memory course that has been used by tens of thousands of people on every continent on earth. It is the Topical Memory System and may be purchased in your local Christian bookstore or by writing to The Navigators, P.O. Box 1659, Colorado Springs, Colo. 80901.

The Old Testament prophet said, "Your iniquities have separated between you and your God" (Isa. 59:2).

3. *Hebrews 9:27:* "And as it is appointed unto men once to die, but after this the judgment." It states that God will hold us accountable for our sins. There is a great judgment day coming. When you are caught speeding there is no use trying to tell the judge that if he'll just forget it you'll try to be good and never do it again. Your violation is on the books, the penalty must be paid. Your sin is on the books before God. He will hold you accountable. And by the way, that's a great verse to share with someone who is confused about reincarnation. We die *once*. I can hear someone saying, "Good grief! All we've heard so far is bad news. We're all sinners, our sins have separated us from God and there is a day of judgment coming." True, but the next verse contains the best news this world has ever heard.

4. *Romans 5:8:* "But God commendeth His love toward us, in that, while we were yet sinners, Christ died for us." The penalty has been paid by Christ. Let's say that you are hauled in front of the judge for speeding and he says, "Thirty dollars or 30 days." You don't have the $30 and it looks bad. But wait! You are struck with amazement and joy at the sight that unfolds. The judge himself lays aside his robes, steps down by your side and pays the penalty for you. That is exactly what God did for us in the Person of His Son, the Lord Jesus Christ. While you and I were yet sinners, Christ died for us.

5. *Ephesians 2:8-9:* "For by grace are ye saved, through faith, and that not of yourselves, it is the gift of God; not of works, lest any man should boast." Salvation is a free gift. Remember, a gift can be accepted or rejected. If it is not accepted, it is rejected. So with God's gracious offer in Christ, we can accept or reject it. If you are thirsty and someone offers you a drink of water, unless you accept it you can die of thirst. It's there, but you must take it.

6. *John 1:12:* "But as many as received Him, to them gave He power to become the sons of God, even to them that believe on His name." We must receive Him into our lives. How? By inviting the risen, living Christ in to live in our hearts, forgive our sins, and give us the free gift of eternal life. Jesus said, "Behold, I stand at the door and knock. If any man hear My voice and open the door, I will come in to him and sup with him, and he with Me" (Rev. 3:20).

As we share these verses and others, the Holy Spirit can use them to draw hearts to the Lord. They will help you make the message clear. But more than that, they contain the truth of the Gospel, the dynamic power of God. The Spirit of God has used these Scriptures to melt the hard hearts and to draw the worst of sinners to a life of righteousness in Christ. Share them in faith and watch with joy as the Holy Spirit uses them to bring life to the lost.

Explaining Regeneration—the New Birth

An important truth you should know and understand as you witness is referred to as regeneration.

When we were in the Holy Land, we enjoyed the time we spent at the Dead Sea. My wife was cautioned twice to be careful not to let any of the water touch her watch or rings. The water is so rich in chemicals that it would ruin them. The sea is beautiful, with the sun shining on it, and with the mountains in the background. It is like some people I know, very rich and very beautiful—but dead!

Have you ever thought about the fact that a Christian is alive in the midst of millions of people who are spiritually dead? The Bible says, "You hath he quickened [brought to life] who were dead in trespasses and sins" (Eph. 2:1).

The Bible is very clear about the fact that the dead can be brought to life. Jesus said, "Except a man be born again, he cannot see the kingdom of God. . . . That which is born of the flesh is flesh, that which is born of the Spirit is spirit. Marvel not that I say unto thee, Ye must be born again" (John 3:3, 6-7). Of course, marvel not! Just as we received physical life by a physical birth, so we receive spiritual life by a spiritual birth.

The Apostle John wrote, "And this is the record, that God hath given us eternal life, and this life is in His Son. He that hath the Son hath life, and he that hath not the Son hath not life" (1 John 5:11-12). Just like the Dead Sea, a person may be rich and beautiful, but without the Lord Jesus Christ he is spiritually dead. Only Jesus can give this life. The imparting of spiritual life is what the theologians refer to as the doctrine of regeneration. The dictionary defines regeneration as "the imparting of spiritual life by divine grace."

Only God can bring life to the dead. The parable of the prodigal son says that he was "dead" but is now "alive" again (Luke 15). Paul says, "That ye put off concerning the former conversation the old man, which is corrupt according to the deceitful lusts. And be renewed in the spirit of your mind; and that ye put on the new man, which after God is created in righteousness and true holiness" (Eph. 4:22-24). Regeneration, the new birth, is the starting point of spiritual growth. Peter said, "As newborn babes, desire the sincere milk of the Word, that ye may grow thereby, if so be ye have tasted that the Lord is gracious" (1 Peter 2:2-3). The dead can be given life, but only by the power of God. That's regeneration.

Helping Another Person Grow Spiritually

Our vegetable garden is a thing of beauty. My wife has a green thumb and loves to dig in the dirt. The lettuce, radishes, corn, tomatoes, and cabbage respond to her tender loving care. Dirt, rain, warm weather, and fertilizer all combine, and soon the plants mature and bear fruit. There is a lot of similarity to what happens in our garden and the spiritual world. The Apostle Paul said, "I have planted, Apollos watered, but God gave the increase" (1 Cor. 3:6).

What traits in our lives provide the best atmosphere to help another grow? *Love* is certainly an important ingredient. "A new commandment I give unto you, that ye love one another; as I have loved you, that ye also love one another. By this shall all men know that ye are My disciples, if ye have love one to another" (John 13:34-35). So by loving others we help them know that God loves them and that His love is not conditional. They don't have to earn it. They couldn't anyway, even if they tried.

Another ingredient is *faith*. Let people see genuine faith in operation. My wife and I had some new Christians around us a few years ago and they got wind of the fact that our financial situation was rather shaky. They came to us and asked us about it. I assured them that we were not worried, that we knew God would provide. Naturally He did. I'm sure that had we been in despair and wringing our hands and worried over the situation, they would have been affected. Later they told us that our example through it had been a real encouragement to them. It bolstered their faith. "But without faith it is impossible to please Him; for he that cometh to God must believe that He is, and that He is a rewarder of them that diligently seek Him" (Heb. 11:6).

Obedience is important. Jesus said, "He that hath My commandments, and keepeth them, he it is that loveth Me; and he that loveth Me shall be loved of My Father, and I will love him, and will manifest Myself to him" (John 14:21). When a young Christian sees instant, complete, and joyful obedience to the Lord lived out before him, it has a powerful effect on his life. There's an old poem, "I'd rather see a sermon than hear one any day; I'd rather someone walk with me than merely point the way." So the example that we set is all important to spiritual growth. Paul said, "Those things which ye have both learned, and received, and heard, and seen in me, do; and the God of peace shall be with you" (Phil. 4:9).

You can help people grow spiritually by getting them into a living vital fellowship with the Lord Jesus through *the Word* and *prayer*. Help them get established in a quiet time. Show them the example of the Lord Jesus. "In the morning, rising up a great while before day, He went out, and departed into a solitary place, and there prayed" (Mark 1:35). One of the best things you can do is have a quiet time with them. Ask if you can come over to their place and spend a few minutes before breakfast reading the Bible and having a time of prayer together. These things are more readily caught than taught. They will learn to do by doing. Show them the importance of Bible study and Bible reading and Scripture memory. Bible reading gives a person the overview of the Bible. Reading regularly through the Word helps tie things together. Bible study lays a foundation in their spiritual lives. Scripture memory gives them the Word of God in the heart, readily available to the Holy Spirit any time, any place. Teach them to pray. Get them into fellowship with other Christians who are involved in these things. This will create desire and prompt faithfulness to the Lord.

I'm sure you see how these relate to your own life. In order to get others started in these practices, you must be doing them consistently yourself. Paul said, "Brethren, be followers together of me, and mark them which walk so as ye have us for an ensample" (Phil. 3:17). If you tell a person, "Here's something that is good for you but personally I never touch it," it will have little effect on his life.

A friend of mine came to Christ while stationed at Pearl Harbor during World War II. He had been a professional gambler and had no Christian background. One of the men in his outfit was a Christian named Ken Waters. Ken had the daily practice of going out to a green, grassy slope, lying down, and spending a few hours in fellowship with the Lord in His Word and prayer. Don assumed that it was the normal thing for Christians to do, so with no fanfare or harangue, he began spending daily time with the Lord in another part of that grassy slope. Ken's life and example provided the impetus for Don.

God can take your life and do the same. Be faithful to Him in daily fellowship and watch with joy and wonder as the Holy Spirit begins to use your life in the lives of others.

Getting Converts into the Word

It was quite a day for me and some of my Christian friends when we received the news. I could tell from the excitement of the man who took the phone call that it was good news. After he hung up, he turned to us and said, "Jerry has surrendered his life to the Lord. Last night he became a Christian." For weeks we had been praying for him, and it was truly a day of rejoicing when the Lord answered.

About a month later our rejoicing turned to concern. During that time various ones of us had had fellowship with Jerry, had prayed with him, and had tried to get across to him the importance of establishing a daily time of fellowship with the Lord, but to no avail. Jerry was a warm, friendly, outgoing young man and was used to sort of sliding by on his personality and glib tongue. He had begun to witness to his fellow pre-med students and tell them of his new-found faith in Christ. Most everyone who knew Jerry liked him and enjoyed being around him, so he found it fairly easy to witness for the Lord. Those of us who had been Christians for some years knew there had to be an intake if the output was to continue, but Jerry was fairly undisciplined and it was going to be tough to get him started in a regular intake of the Word or to help him establish a time of prayer.

Then it happened. I first heard about it from a young Christian who lived on the same floor in the dorm. One night about 10 of Jerry's friends had come into his room and had begun to give him "the business" about his faith. They asked him questions; they had all kinds of arguments against the Bible; some questioned the existence of God; others pointed out all the fun he had been missing. They were out to shake him up and they spent about three hours with him questioning, laughing, mocking, and arguing.

Jerry was shook. Then his zeal began to cool. He began to hang around the old gang again. After a while some of the old habits began to reappear. He occasionally went to church, but when we talked to him he told us he didn't want to become a fanatic. He drifted off into that bland, pure vanilla brand of Christianity that has lukewarmness as its standard, the kind that is so disgusting to God. "I know thy works, that thou art neither cold nor hot; I would thou wert cold or hot. So then, because thou art lukewarm, and neither cold nor hot, I will spew thee out of My mouth" (Rev. 3:15-16).

Jerry's problem was simple, and his story is being repeated constantly all over the world. I recall a young football player who met the Lord and began to go all over the state giving his testimony for Christ. He was so busy he didn't have time to get down to business in his daily walk with Christ. Fortunately, he realized what was happening, sought out some help, and today is the pastor of a dynamic, soul-winning church. Jesus explained the problem. "These are they likewise which are sown on stony ground, who, when they have heard the Word, immediately receive it with gladness, and have no root in themselves, and so endure but for a time; afterward, when affliction or persecution ariseth for the Word's sake, immediately they are offended" (Mark 4:16-17).

The person who relies on his experience or his personality to carry him through is in for a shock. When the devil strikes, the Word of God is our best defense. It is wonderful to see men and women take off like rockets when they are converted to Christ. It's wonderful to see them serving the Lord, testifying to His saving grace, and being active in Christian things.

However, there must be a behind-the-scenes fellowship with Christ if it is to last. Here is the way Luke tells it. "They on the rock are they which, when they hear, receive the Word with joy; and these have no root, which for a while believe, and in time of temptation fall away. And that which fell among thorns are they which, when they have heard, go forth, and are choked with cares and riches and pleasures of this life, and bring no fruit to perfection" (Luke 8:13-14). But the story can have a happy ending, as in the case of the football player. "But that on the good ground are they, which in an honest and good heart, having heard the Word, keep it, and bring forth fruit with patience" (8:15).

Prologue to Chapter 9

As I look back over the years and think of the keen young Christian men and women I have known who are not walking with the Lord today, it becomes evident that the path is fraught with hazards and dangers that are very real. There is no use trying to kid ourselves. We have a formidable enemy who will stop at nothing, and who will employ every means at his disposal to thwart our progress in Christ. To be forewarned is to be forearmed.

I can't emphasize too strongly the need to watch for the danger signs as they may appear in your spiritual life. Some of the material in this chapter comes from my own sad experiences, and some from the lives of people who have fallen into the devil's snare. These pages go out with the prayer that you may be spared some of the heartache that goes with stumbling along the path.

9

The Hazards of Discipleship

One night each week my friend used to go downtown to the bus depot and share Christ with the servicemen who gathered there. Through this effort many of them had come to know the Lord. Later I heard someone criticize him for carrying on his activities in the strength and energy of the flesh. When I heard it, I asked Skip, another friend of mine, what he thought about the accusations. Skip said he thought such accusations were straight from the pit of hell. I agreed. Surely, there is a place for diligent, persistent, regular witness.

The Work of the Flesh

An important point to remember arises here. It *is* possible to carry on work for the Lord in the power and motivation of the flesh. It often shows up when a person is overly concerned about making a good impression. "Menpleasing" is as old as the New Testament. The Apostle Paul spoke of serving "in singleness of your heart, as unto Christ, not with eyeservice as menpleasers; but as the servants of Christ, doing the will of God from the heart, with good will doing service, as to the Lord, and not to men" (Eph. 6:5-7).

Menpleasing often shows up within the activities of the church. The young Sunday School teacher wants desperately to do a good job in order to please the superintendent. The young pastor tries to make a good impression on those over him in the denomination. I watched a young campus minister go out on his first assignment and practically work himself to death in his desire to please his regional director. His first year was characterized by long hours, nervous tension, inner struggles, and an abundance of hard work and striving in the energies of human wisdom and strength. Though pride is often lurking behind the scenes in situations like this, it wasn't in this case. It was simply a desire to do a good job and please his immediate superior for whom he had the highest regard. So he worked himself to a frazzle. It is interesting to note that just as laziness and sloth can be deadly in the life of a Christian, working too hard and trying with all of your might can be equally dangerous.

I mentioned that pride was not the motivating force behind the young campus minister, but it is in many cases. Jesus warned, "Take heed that ye do not your alms before men, to be seen by them; otherwise ye have no reward of your Father which is in heaven" (Matt. 6:1). Something in all of us desires to be seen, to be talked about, to be praised. That something is pride, and it can be the thing that sets off a flurry of activity, long hours, and sleepless nights. The devil is a master at playing on our weaknesses and keeping us off balance. He comes to us and says, "Slow down!" I can't slow down. "OK," he says, "speed up!" It doesn't matter to him. Either way he can trick us into a situation that is basically unproductive.

Another thing that can be behind all the hard work is the desire to be like someone else. We see the person, admire him, and try to be like him. It is true that the Apostle Paul taught the doctrine of pacesetting. "Those things which ye have both learned, and received, and heard, and seen in me, do, and the God of peace shall be with you" (Phil. 4:9). He was speaking about his love for Christ, concern for the lost, and burden to help fellow Christians mature in Christ. These God-given desires should be in all of us. The danger comes when we try to do things the same way another person does them, without regard to the gifts and abilities that God may have given us. The person we admire is, no doubt, exercising his God-given gifts in the strength of the Holy Spirit. Unless we use our own gifts we will be in trouble. If God gave the gift, we must use it.

When God made us He did so with many fine balances. This is one of them. Sloth and striving are both unscriptural. The key is to rest in the Lord and labor in the strength that God gives.

Laziness (Sloth)

You can destroy your life in many ways. You may choose an objective, strive to attain it, work day and night, and at the end of your life discover you gave your life to the wrong thing. I've met and talked with men who have done that. It's a tragic thing. They've looked at me and said, "LeRoy, I've wasted my life. I've worked and struggled and now I can look back and see I was on the wrong track. My life has amounted to nothing."

You can destroy your life by never giving yourself to anything. You become a dabbler. Your motto is, "These 40 things I dabble at" rather than "This one thing I do." Your life is like a moth at a theater marquee. You flit from one thing to another and never really accomplish anything. At the end you look back and nothing has been done. Your life has been wasted chasing one illusion after another.

A third way to have your life count for nothing is to give in to that lazy streak that's in most of us and do nothing. The Bible has a great deal to say about each of these.

The Scriptures give tremendous promises to the person who wants to get on the right track and stay there. "For this God is our God forever and ever; He will be our guide even unto death" (Ps. 48:14). If you have been on the wrong track, God promises to lead you into His perfect will. If you have been wasting your life jumping from this to that, God promises to set you in the perfect way. "Trust in the Lord with all thine heart, and lean not unto thine own understanding. In all thy ways acknowledge Him, and He shall direct thy paths" (Prov. 3:5-6). However, to the slothful, lazy person God gives nothing but warnings. In fact, the Book of Proverbs abounds with them.

"Go to the ant, thou sluggard; consider her ways, and be wise, which, having no guide, overseer, or ruler, provideth her food in the summer, and gathereth her food in the harvest. How long wilt thou sleep, O sluggard? When wilt thou arise out of thy sleep? Yet a little sleep, a little slumber, a little folding of the hands to sleep, so shall thy poverty come like one that travelleth and thy want like an armed man" (Prov. 6:6-11). The lesson is simple. Sloth will lead to disaster. If the ant did not work and plan for the future, it would starve. God, in His Word, condemns anxious worry about the future, but here He commends wise foresight. Hard work is portrayed as a virtue, and idleness is shown to be a vice. Jesus spoke of the man who buried his talent as wicked as well as slothful (Matt. 25:26).

I have watched the effects of sloth in the spiritual realm. I know a fellow who admires those who are deep in the Word of God but he will not study. He enjoys the fellowship of those who have made their heart the library of Christ, but he will not pay the price of Scripture memory. He thrills to hear of an abundant answer to prayer, but he will not labor in prayer. He is the living testimony to the truth of Proverbs 21:25: "The desire of the slothful killeth him; for his hands refuse to labor." One of the sins of Sodom was an "abundance of idleness" (Ezek. 16:49).

If you have found yourself slipping into the trap of slothfulness and have caught yourself giving in to your lazy streak, there are a couple of things you can do. One is to memorize a verse or two from the Book of Proverbs in which the Lord speaks about sloth. This will enable the Holy Spirit to speak to you about it throughout the day. The other thing I suggest is that you frequently offer a prayer to God to deliver you from this evil. Sloth will destroy your life. "The fool foldeth his hands together, and eateth his own flesh" (Ecc. 4:5).

The Tongue

It's really easy to get into trouble. You may hear something you're not supposed to hear, or see something you're not supposed to see. Your feet can take you to places you're not supposed to go and your hands can help you do things you're not supposed to do. But of all your members that can get you into trouble—your eyes, ears, hands, feet—the one to watch out for is your tongue.

When I was a freshman at Northwestern College in Minneapolis, one of our instructors had us memorize James 3:5-6: "Even so the tongue is a little member, and boasteth great things. Behold, how great a matter a little fire kindleth! And the tongue is a fire, a world of iniquity; so is the tongue among our members, that it defileth the whole body, and setteth on fire the course of nature, and it is set on fire of hell." I really didn't understand her concern at the time, but as the years have passed I have begun to see what she was getting at. She was warning us about the troubles our tongue could produce.

During my summer vacation between my sophomore and junior years I went to a conference in California. The speaker was Dawson Trotman and in one of his messages he spoke on dangers to the Christian life. To my surprise, the tongue was at the top of the list.

Recently I received a letter from a missionary family in Africa. The wife told of the difficulties of mailing a letter. The Post Office had been out of the proper stamps for months. She wrote, "Unthinkingly, I quipped an impatient remark about it to my husband. He smiled and said, 'Sweetie, I think you need to learn to do all things without murmurings and disputings.' I thought, *That's right.*" She went on to tell how the Lord had spoken to her the next morning from His Word. As I read the letter I thought how easy it is to fall into a grumbling and complaining spirit. It is a deadly habit, not only because it brings a dark and gloomy atmosphere to everyone around us, but it is a form of unbelief and rebellion against God. When we complain, we show that we really don't believe He is in control of our lives.

It creates another problem also. Just as it is hard to get the feathers back in the pillow and the toothpaste back into the tube, so it is hard to get a work spoken hastily or in anger off the record. Once it's said, it's said. James wrote, "But the tongue can no man tame; it is an unruly evil, full of deadly poison. Therewith bless we God, even the Father; and therewith curse we men, who are made after the similitude of God. Out of the same mouth proceed blessing and cursing. My brethren, these things ought not so to be" (James 3:8-10). It is so much easier to explode and shoot off our mouths than to keep quiet or respond with a soft answer that will help to calm the anger. The Bible teaches that a mark of maturity is to say the right thing at the right time in the right way. "If any man offend not in word, the same is a perfect [mature] man, and able to bridle the whole body" (James 3:2).

Other dangers of the tongue are recorded in Proverbs. One of the passages speaks against a practice into which many of us have fallen. How often do we find ourselves maligning someone? Cutting someone down can be done as a joke, but all too often it has as its real motive the desire to make ourselves look good by comparison. The Bible speaks against this. "There is that speaketh like the piercings of a sword, but the tongue of the wise is health" (Prov. 12:18).

The tongue can be used to stir up strife between friends. "He that covereth a transgression seeketh love, but he that repeateth a matter separateth friends" (Prov. 17:9). "A froward [perverse] man soweth strife, and a whisperer separateth chief friends" (16:28). The Bible speaks of "wholesome words" and "words without knowledge." The Christian will do well to make his speech a matter of daily prayer, and to study the life of the Lord Jesus who astounded people "at the gracious words that proceeded out of His mouth" (Luke 4:22).

Living with Bitterness

"Mounds of health" is a family favorite of ours. That's the name we've given soybean pancakes topped with yogurt and fresh blueberries. We had them last Sunday when we returned home from church. I was wearing a new pair of trousers I had received for my birthday and as I scooped the blueberries on the pancakes I was very careful not to spill any on the new pants. It would have left a stain that would have been extremely difficult, if not impossible, to remove. It would have been like the blue ink that's on my white shirt. Because the shirt went through the washer with a ball-point pen in the pocket, the ink spots will never come out of the material.

The Scripture warns about problems like that. "Follow peace with all men, and holiness, without which no man shall see the Lord, looking diligently lest any man fail of the grace of God, lest any root of bitterness springing up trouble you, and by it many be defiled" (Heb. 12:14-15). Here's an exhortation to live at peace with everybody, even those who are giving you a hard time. That's difficult to do, but Jesus was clear on this point. "Blessed are ye, when men shall revile you, and persecute you, and shall say all manner of evil against you falsely, for My sake. Rejoice, and be exceedingly glad; for great is your reward in heaven; for so persecuted they the prophets who were before you" (Matt. 5:11-12).

The option is ours. We can live a blessed, happy life with a full reward in heaven, or we can endure our days in bitterness, failing of the grace of God. The problem with the latter is that it not only ruins your own life, but defiles and stains everything and everyone it touches. It is like a plague that spreads through the land, fouling and crippling everyone in its path. A bitter spirit produces bitter fruit in the person's own life and in the life of others. The person is in a precarious position when he carries about a bitter spirit. God cannot pour His grace into a life that is filled with bitterness.

Why? Because a bitter person has denied the sovereignty of God. Quite possibly such a person has been wronged and has been wounded in spirit. If he grows bitter as a result, he denies the truth that all things do, in fact, work together for good to them that love God. He ignores the Bible's command to "rejoice evermore" (1 Thes. 5:16), and give thanks in everything. And he is locking himself into a course that will end ultimately in destruction. His bitter spirit may defile many others, but it will destroy him.

Maybe you've had it happen to you. Someone was unkind, unthoughtful, or mean. He said something or did something that hurt you deeply. Don't harbor it in resentment. Don't let it grow into bitterness. Go to the person and get it all out on the table. Forgive, forget, and face the future with an unfailing supply of the grace of God. If you don't, you'll be the big loser in the end. Remember the words of Jesus: "Moreover, if thy brother shall trespass against thee, go and tell him his fault between thee and him alone; if he shall hear thee, thou hast gained thy brother" (Matt. 18:15).

Living with Suffering

It is really an awesome thing to stand in the Garden of Gethsemane, which is located right at the foot of the Mount of Olives. The olive trees are now over 2,000 years old. It is a beautiful setting, but it isn't the beauty of the place that overwhelms you. It's the history. It's what went on there. The word *Gethsemane* means "olive oil press." An olive oil press is constructed so that two huge round rough stones grind against each other, and there's a groove cut in one of them for the oil to run out. Because of the weight of the stones, tremendous pressure is put on the olives.

Those of us who have read of the sufferings and agony of Christ in that garden know that the greatest pressure experienced there was not physical pressure but spiritual. His soul was exceeding sorrowful, even unto death. He was in agony and His sweat was "as it were great drops of blood falling to the ground" (Luke 22:44). Here was agony, suffering, and spiritual pressure that was unique in the annals of history. It is also true that the followers of Christ have been promised a taste of that pressure.

Peter said, "Beloved, think it not strange concerning the fiery trial which is to try you, as though some strange thing happened unto you" (1 Peter 4:12). Paul stated, "For unto you it is given in the behalf of Christ, not only to believe on Him, but also to suffer for His sake" (Phil. 1:29). Jesus said, "These things I have spoken unto you, that in Me ye might have peace. In the world ye shall have tribulation, but be of good cheer; I have overcome the world" (John 16:33). How do we handle it? What do we do?

First, there must be a determination to endure our sufferings courageously. Long before the agony of the garden, Jesus began to teach His disciples that He must suffer many things and be killed. When the time came, He steadfastly set His face to go to Jerusalem. He was determined to see it through. Second, there must be a commitment to the will of God. Jesus prayed, "Not My will but Thine be done" (Luke 22:42). In the midst of it all, there must be earnest prayer. The record tells us that Jesus prayed earnestly. Third, there must be a realistic view of the trials and pressures we face. In speaking of this, Paul said, "We . . . do groan, being burdened" (2 Cor. 5:4). These are groans of sorrow under a heavy load. We need to realize that the calamities of life are a heavy load. There is no use trying to deceive ourselves that this should not be. For a person to think that just because he is a Christian, he will not face suffering is not true. Facts prove otherwise.

But our suffering must be examined in light of heaven. "For our light affliction, which is but for a moment, worketh for us a far more exceeding and eternal weight of glory. While we look not at the things which are seen, but at the things which are not seen; for the things which are seen are temporal; but the things which are not seen are eternal" (2 Cor. 4:17-18). We know that we have a home awaiting us, eternal in the heavens. Thank God for that living hope, because where there is hope, life has meaning and purpose.

We have all read of prisoners of war whose lives drained away when they lost hope of being released. Peter said, "Blessed be the God and Father of our Lord Jesus Christ, which according to His abundant mercy hath begotten us again unto a lively hope by the resurrection of Jesus Christ from the dead, to an inheritance incorruptible, and undefiled, and that fadeth not away, reserved in heaven for you, who are kept by the power of God through faith unto salvation ready to be revealed in the last time. Wherein ye greatly rejoice, though now for a season if need be, ye are in heaviness through manifold temptations, that the trial of your faith, being much more precious than of gold that perisheth, though it be tried with fire, might be found unto praise and honor and glory at the appearing of Jesus Christ. Whom having not seen, ye love; in whom though now ye see Him not, yet believing, ye rejoice with joy unspeakable and full of glory, receiving the end of your faith, even the salvation of your souls" (1 Peter 1:3-9).

Pressure is a fact of life with which Christian and non-Christian alike must live. The difference is that the non-Christian has no invisible means of support. The Christian has the promise of God to bolster him and the Spirit of God to make them live in his soul. The hymnwriter spoke of this when he penned, "Are ye weak and heavy laden, / burdened with a load of care? / Precious Saviour, still our refuge, / take it to the Lord in prayer." Why? Because Jesus faced it and can help us in time of need. "Who in the days of His flesh, when He had offered up prayers and supplications with strong crying and tears unto Him that was able to save Him from death, and was heard in that He feared; though He were a Son, yet learned He obedience by the things which He suffered; and being made perfect, He became the author of eternal salvation unto all them that obey Him" (Heb. 5:7-9).

Missionaries sometimes have to be sent home because they can't live with pressure. Bank presidents resign, teachers quit, people drop out of public office. Some people turn to alcohol or drugs. Pressure is the bully that drives thousands off the street of their dreams and aspirations and sends them down the blind alley of despair. In the New Testament it goes under many names: affliction, torment, hardship, suffering, and others. None of these are pretty words. The average person would look at any one of them and rather not meet them face to face. But the Lord promises in His Word, that these ugly intruders can really be angels in disguise, who direct us into the presence of Him Who has the solution to our problems of pressure.

Living with Your Past

From the potter's field outside Jerusalem we could look up and see the palace of Caiaphas the high priest. As I stood in the field, purchased with the 30 pieces of silver that had been paid to Judas when he betrayed Christ, I thought of the destinies of the two men associated with these places: Judas who betrayed the Lord, and Peter who denied Him at the palace of the high priest. Both of them spent the night in weeping.

With Judas it was the double tragedy of infamy and death. He betrayed Jesus and then went out and hanged himself. But with Peter it was different. Certainly he had denied the Lord. It was an act of cowardice that could have ruined his life. He could have been crushed with guilt and remorse for the rest of his days. But he wasn't. Why? Because by the grace of God, he found the place of repentance and confession, and was used of God to write two books of the Bible and lead thousands to Christ.

The Bible is full of stories of men whose lives could have been ruined by a single act. Mark, who left Paul and Barnabas and went home during the first missionary journey, could have spent the rest of his life in self-justification and condemnation. He could have spent his life defending what he had done as being right, or he could have been eaten alive with regret because he knew it was wrong. But neither happened. He later proved profitable in the ministry and was used of God to write one of the four Gospels.

Think about that for a minute! An unfaithful servant of Christ used of God to present to the world the Lord Jesus as the faithful servant of God. Mark's life is another instance where tragedy turned to triumph. Time would fail to tell of David, whose sins brought death and tragedy, but he became the man after God's own heart. Paul could have been plagued by the question, "How could God use a murderer" as he reflected on the days when he slaughtered the followers of Christ.

Perhaps you have something in your past that the devil uses to keep you from being the man or woman that God wants you to be. The Apostle Paul said, "Brethren, I count not myself to have apprehended, but this one thing I do, forgetting those things which are behind, and reaching forth unto those things which are before, I press toward the mark for the prize of the high calling of God in Christ Jesus" (Phil. 3:13-14). Forget those things which are behind. Don't dwell on the past.

Find the blessed peace of repentance and cleansing of God. Accept the forgiveness and cleansing of God by faith. Put your life in God's hands and press toward the mark of the high calling of God in Christ Jesus. It may not be easy. Very few good things are.

Paul said, "I press toward the mark," and the word *press* always indicates resistance. He didn't say, "I float toward the mark; I drift or slide." He said "I press!" It may be tough, but it *is* possible to forget those things which are behind. We know, because the Bible teaches that we can choose what we will think about. "Whatsoever things are true, whatsoever things are honest, whatsoever things are just, whatsoever things are pure, whatsoever things are lovely, whatsoever things are of good report; if there be any virtue, and if there be any praise; think on these things" (Phil. 4:8). Paul gave a list of virtues and then instructed us to think on these things. It is possible, therefore, to choose what your mind will dwell on. Otherwise we would not have been commanded to do it. The Bible doesn't give commands that are impossible to obey.

Many Christians are unaware of the fact that one of the devil's master strokes is to immobilize us with regret and remorse over something which is over and done with. It works like this: We recognize our sin and guilt, and confess it to God with an honest desire to repent. At that moment God cleanses and forgives. The Bible says that He casts our sins into the depths of the sea (Micah 7:19), removes them as far as the east is from the west (Ps. 103:12), and remembers them no more (Isa. 43:25). He forgets them.

But the devil does not forget. He comes to us with his deceit and lies and calls our attention to them again. Once again we are smitten with remorse and slip into the mire of despondency. And so it goes. Our memory becomes the devil's playground. In the Scripture he is called the accuser of the brethren and he does this day and night. Especially at night. Many a good night's sleep is lost to his accusations.

Christian, believe God. "If we confess our sins, He is faithful and just to forgive us our sins, and to cleanse us from all unrighteousness" (1 John 1:9). Accept that promise and wake up to a new day of victory and usefulness in the kingdom of God.

Prologue to Chapter 10

The Book of Genesis gives us an account of Adam and Eve and their fall into sin (Gen. 3). On the surface it might appear that it was their appetite for food that caused them to fall. A closer look, however, shows that their temptation was complete: "For all that is in the world, the lust of the flesh, and the lust of the eyes, and the pride of life, is not of the Father, but is of the world" (1 John 2:16). The record states, "When the woman saw that the tree was good for food [the lust of the flesh], and that it was pleasant to the eyes [lust of the eyes—covetousness], and a tree to be desired to make one wise [pride of life], she took of the fruit thereof, and did eat, and gave also unto her husband with her; and he did eat" (Gen. 3:6). So the first Adam was tempted, and failed spiritually.

The temptation of Christ was also complete, as we see in the Gospel records (Matt. 4; Luke 4). Satan tempted Him to make bread from stones (lust of the flesh), tempted Him with ownership of all that the devil showed Him (lust of the eyes), and tempted Him to cast Himself off the temple to show openly that heaven's angels could protect Him (an appeal to the pride of life). So Jesus, the last Adam, was tempted, and came away victorious.

This chapter points out that the way to victory is through Him who was the first victor over sin and Satan.

10

Victory Over Sin

If you ever want to get some good advice on how to make a million dollars, don't go down to skid row and get your instructions from some beggar sitting there with a tin cup in his hand. Jesus is the One who triumphed. So if we want to learn how to live in victory, we must go to the One who is victorious, namely, Jesus Himself.

The Source of Victory

Satan, at one time, had been in the very presence of God enjoying the splendors of heaven. Bible scholars have described him as heaven's choirmaster. But he rebelled against God and soon found himself crawling on his belly eating the dust of the earth. He knew from personal experience that going the way of sin and rebellion only leads to disaster. The Bible says, "Every man is tempted, when he is drawn away of his own lust, and enticed" (James 1:14). Drawn away from what? From God. When we're drawn away from God, from His presence, His fellowship, and His Word, we are drawn away into our own lusts and thus are tempted. It was like that in the Garden of Eden, when Eve decided to follow the advice of the devil. How foolish! To follow the instructions of one who was absolutely bankrupt!

Two words are keys to spiritual victory: *life* and *death*. One of the great chapters on victory in the Christian life (Rom. 6) has one of the two prominent words in it: "God forbid. How shall we, that are *dead* to sin, live any longer therein?" (v. 2). The teaching is clear. We are to live no longer in sin. The Apostle Peter put it this way, "Forasmuch then as Christ hath suffered for us in the flesh, arm yourselves likewise with the same mind, for he that hath suffered in the flesh hath ceased from sin; that he no longer should live the rest of his time in the flesh to the lusts of men, but to the will of God. For the time past of our life may suffice us to have wrought the will of the Gentiles, when we walked in lasciviousness, lusts, excess of wine, revellings, banquetings, and abominable idolatries" (1 Peter 4:1-3).

Paul says, "Know ye not, that so many of us as were baptized into Jesus Christ were baptized into His death?" (Rom. 6:3) The principle is to get the old habits weakened through lack of use. The word *destroyed* has the idea of being rendered unemployed, put out of work. In light of that, "Let not sin therefore reign in your mortal body, that ye should obey it in the lusts thereof" (6:12). Sin must not reign. It may remain as an outlaw remains in the land, making an occasional strike and doing occasional damage; but it must not reign. It must not make the laws, chair the meetings, or command the army.

The second keyword of victory is to be *alive* unto God, to walk in newness of life. "Therefore we are buried with Him by baptism into death; that like as Christ was raised up from the dead by the glory of the Father, even so we also should walk in newness of life" (Rom. 6:4). As Christians we learn to walk by new rules, choosing new paths toward new goals.

Most of the troublesome issues of life that vex the Christian are not settled once and for all. For that reason the Apostle Paul says, "Neither yield ye your members as instruments of unrighteousness unto sin, but yield yourselves unto God, as those that are alive from the dead, and your members as instruments of righteousness unto God. For sin shall not have dominion over you; for ye are not under the law, but under grace" (Rom. 6:13-14). So we yield ourselves, not as losers to a victor, but as eager students to an all-wise teacher. "I beseech you therefore, brethren, by the mercies of God, that ye present your bodies a living sacrifice, holy, acceptable unto God, which is your reasonable service" (Rom. 12:1).

Enemies of Our Soul

People are often defeated in the spiritual battles of life because they don't know the rules for victory. God in His Word has revealed these rules in clear and unmistakable statements. They should be studied and followed with all diligence. Battles are not won by lectures on gunpowder, but as we meet the enemy and overcome him. The Christian is constantly at war; he has three enemies ever against him: the world, the flesh, and the devil. Each of these enemies of our souls must be met and defeated in different ways and with different weapons.

The world, with all the allurements, all of its froth and tinsel, all of its empty praise, is a powerful foe and must be faced seriously. Our weapon is fellowship with Christ. The little song says, "And the things of earth will grow strangely dim in the light of His glory and grace." We need to maintain a daily time of fellowship with Christ (see chaps. 2-4). Our faith grows through fellowship with Him. The Bible says, "For whatsoever is born of God overcometh the world, and this is the victory that overcometh the world, even our faith" (1 John 5:4).

We overcome the temptations of the flesh by fleeing. Paul told Timothy, "Flee also youthful lusts" (2 Tim. 2:22). Solomon wrote, "My son, if sinners entice thee, consent thou not. Walk not thou in the way with them. Refrain thy foot from their path. Avoid it, pass not by it, turn from it, and pass away" (Prov. 1:10, 15; 4:15). So much flammable material exists in our fleshly desires that it is foolish to even get near the sparks. God told Eve that there was one tree in the garden to avoid. And where do we find her? Sitting directly under it. Alone! Not too bright.

The third enemy we face is the *devil.* In doing battle with him, we fight; we don't give him an inch, because he doesn't deserve it. The Bible says, "Resist the devil, and he will flee from you" (James 4:7); "Greater is he that is in you, than he that is in the world" (1 John 4:4). In fighting the devil, the weapons of our warfare are not carnal, but mighty through God. We use God's Word, which is living and powerful. As we saturate our lives with the Word of God, the blessed Holy Spirit uses that Word because it is His Sword. Paul said, "And take . . . the sword of the Spirit, which is the Word of God" (Eph. 6:17). Jesus set the example on the mount of temptation when He used the Word of God to defeat the devil. By using the Word as our weapon, we are, rather than fighting in our own energy, claiming the victory Christ has already won for us when He defeated Satan at Calvary.

So then, just as in the physical sense we use different weapons to fight different enemies (you don't fight a thief in a dark alley with a submarine!) so the Christian has specific weapons for the different enemies he faces. The flesh? We flee. The world? We fellowship with Jesus. The devil? We fight.

Misconceptions of Victory

Some battles you can't win. I was on a plane from Dallas to Colorado Springs and watched a guy fight a losing battle all the way. He was in the seat in front of me. I was sitting in the row with the emergency exit and as you know, the seats in front of that row can't be reclined. If they were pushed back they would block that row and regulations forbid blocking the row with the emergency exit. This man didn't know that, and for 700 miles he pushed the seat recline button again and again. He strained and lunged against the seat, but to no avail. He fought a losing battle.

Many earnest Christians fight just such a losing battle trying to live a victorious life because of any one of six common misconceptions of the way victory is won. These misconceptions sound good, appear logical, and can be preached from the pulpit with zeal and fervor. As the unsuspecting child of God embraces the faulty idea presented and applies it, becomes confused and discouraged.

Misconception 1: Confession is victory. Confession is *not* a way to experience victory. But it *is* the way we restore fellowship. "If we confess our sins, He is faithful and just to forgive us our sins, and to cleanse us from all unrighteousness" (1 John 1:9). Through confession we take the initial step and God is pleased. It is only a beginning; it does not take us all the way down the triumphant path.

Misconception 2: We must beg God for victory. Night after night, day after day, one church service after another, the person realizes his failure and beseeches God for victory. He may go forward to an altar of prayer or kneel at his own bed. The thing he doesn't realize is that when we ask God for victory, this prayer cannot be answered because victory for the believer has already been won. Jesus has triumphed over sin and death, over the world, the flesh, and the devil. "But thanks be to God, who giveth us the victory through our Lord Jesus Christ" (1 Cor. 15:57). The exciting truth is that the victorious Christ lives within us, and it is

God's desire that we rely solely on the relationship we already have with Him.

Misconception 3: We need to ask God for something more. We err when we think that God needs to add something to us before we can experience the victorious Christian life. The Bible says, "Blessed be the God and Father of our Lord Jesus Christ, who hath blessed us with all spiritual blessings in heavenly places in Christ" (Eph. 1:3). What more can we possibly need if we already possess every blessing that heaven contains? The person with Jesus Christ in his heart has all the resources he needs, "For in Him [Christ] dwelleth all the fullness of the Godhead bodily. And ye are complete in Him, which is the head of all principality and power" (Col. 2:9-10). When God declares us complete in Christ, to say we need something more is to blaspheme the name of Christ, deny the work of Christ, and ridicule the power of Christ. When we are yielded to Him, we are filled with the fulness of the triune God: the fullness of the Father, Son, and Holy Spirit.

Misconception 4: Victory is self-discipline. We need to be tough on ourselves. Obviously discipline has its place in the life of the disciple, but our human efforts won't lead to victory. Paul taught, "Wherefore, if ye be dead with Christ from the rudiments of the world, why, as though living in the world, are ye subject to ordinances (touch not; taste not; handle not; which all are to perish with the using) after the commandments and doctrines of men? Which things have indeed a show of wisdom in will-worship, and humility, and neglecting of the body, not in any honor to the satisfying of the flesh" (Col. 2:20-23).

Misconception 5: Victory is maturity. We get better as we grow older. True maturity does not make us more victorious, but it does bring us to a place of greater humility and more reliance on the grace of God. Peter describes what happened to us when we were born again into God's family: "Whereby are given unto us exceeding great and precious promises, that by these ye might be partakers of the divine nature, having escaped the corruption that is in the world through lust" (2 Peter 1:4). Maturity simply means our new man is being renewed day by day and our old fleshly nature, which cannot be improved, is losing control.

Misconception 6: Victory is simply trying to do the right things. Trying to do the right thing as a way of "achieving" victory is what we call legalism. Paul asked, "This only would I learn of you, received ye the Spirit by the works of the law, or by the hearing of faith? Are ye so foolish? Having begun in the Spirit, are ye now made perfect by the flesh?" (Gal. 3:2-3) We should not depend on any activity, no matter how "spiritual," to raise us to a level of greater devotion and consistent victory except as a means of getting to know God, who, in the final analysis, is all we need. Activities do not bring spiritual victory. We are fighting a losing battle if we travel that road. Victory is found in the victorious Christ, and in Him alone.

Lust, the Sin of Impurity

Though I haven't seen him in years, I can remember my conversations with him as though they were yesterday. He was such an impressive young man: tall, handsome, well-mannered, intelligent, spiritual. Like Jesus, he was growing "in wisdom and stature, and in favor with God and man." The summer after we met he was working on the staff of a Christian organization. That autumn he went back to college, with a personal invitation from the president of the mission to return next summer. Everyone was challenged and impressed.

That autumn he attended a conference where I was speaking, and I could sense there was something wrong. His eye had lost its sparkle, his face had lost its smile, and his step had lost its bounce. He avoided me. He kept to himself. After the last meeting I sought him out and asked some questions. Had I done something to offend him? Was there something I needed to apologize for?

"No," he said, "it was nothing like that."

I was relieved, and because I felt he really didn't want to talk, I was about to leave when he began to spill it all out. It seems that after the summer he had met a girl. Her husband traveled a lot and she was lonesome. Soon he was spending time over at her home, and before long he was living in sin with her.

His story reminded me of another one—in Proverbs. Here was a young man walking down the street who met a girl. She played up to him and caught him with her attractive clothes and fair speech. Soon he went home with her to take his fill of love. Her husband was away on a long journey and she was in need of companionship. Here's how the story ends: "With her much fair speech she caused him to yield; with the flattering of her lips she forced him. He goeth after her straightway, as an ox goeth to the slaughter, or as a fool to the correction of the stocks, till an arrow strike through his liver, as a bird hasteth to the snare, and knoweth not that it is for his life. Hearken unto me now, therefore, O ye children, and attend to the words of my mouth. Let not thine heart decline to her ways; go not astray in her paths. For she hath cast down many wounded; yea, many strong men have been slain by her. Her house is the way to hell, going down to the chambers of death" (Prov. 7:21-27).

Two or three truths stand out in this story. Though the victim is a young man, void of understanding, the record is plain that many strong men have been slain by her as well. It is not only the young and foolish who fall into the sin of the lust of the flesh. Strong Christians, pastors, and missionaries have fallen as well. Our young man in this story apparently had some stability and resisted for a while, for it says, "With much fair speech she caused him to yield."

But here's the frightening thing. The writer of Proverbs, who told this story and gave these clear warnings, fell into this same sin. "Did Solomon, king of Israel, sin by these things? Yet among many nations was there no king like him, who was beloved of his God, and God made him king over all Israel; nevertheless, even him did outlandish women cause to sin" (Neh. 13:26).

Even though Timothy was a colaborer with the Apostle Paul, a strong young disciple who had abandoned the way of the world for a life of service for Christ, Paul thought it necessary to warn him to flee youthful lusts and to replace them with righteousness, faith, love, and peace, and find companionship with those who call on the Lord out of a pure heart (see 2 Tim. 2:22). Had my friend been enmeshed in the love of God rather than the lust of the flesh, he would have been preserved.

Righteousness and faith are powerful weapons against the lusts of youth. When you find yourself in the way of this temptation, the wise thing to do is to depart and flee. This temptation is deadly. "Wherefore, let him that thinketh he standeth take heed lest he fall" (1 Cor. 10:12).

Lust, the Sin of Worldliness
The dream of every singer, juggler, actor, comedian, magician,

and acrobat in show business was to reach Broadway! The lights, money, fame, and the crowds and excitement drew them like a kitten is drawn to catnip. If they could play Broadway they had it made. They had arrived. They had hit the summit. In looking for the good life, Broadway was the way to go.

But the history of show business is filled with an interesting conclusion. Most of those who strove for Broadway soon discovered that it was not what they had thought it would be. Their dreams, hopes, and aspirations were often shattered in bitter disappointment. The lights dimmed. The fame faded. The crowds thinned, and from then on it was all downhill.

The Bible also mentions a broad way, and it also leads to bitter disappointment. In fact, it is Jesus Himself who speaks of this. "Enter ye in at the narrow gate; for wide is the gate, and broad is the way, that leadeth to destruction, and many there be who go in that way, because narrow is the gate, and narrow is the way which leadeth unto life, and few there be that find it" (Matt. 7:13-14). Many people in our modern, pleasure-mad, sophisticated society would question that truth. That statement applies to our life here and now as well as to our eternal destiny. The gate of salvation is narrow. There are not many roads that lead to heaven. Jesus said, "I am the way, the truth, and the life; no man cometh unto the Father, but by Me" (John 14:6).

It is also true that the good life here and now is found in following the narrow way rather than the broad way. One leads to life—abundant life. The other leads to destruction.

Is it really true that committing your life to one mate for life is better than playing house with a dozen? Is it really true that abiding by the Ten Commandments is better than making up your own rules as you go along? Is it really true that Jesus knew more about life and how it should be lived than all our modern sociologists, psychologists, and late night talk show celebrities?

Those who traveled the broad way and then turned to the narrow path are unanimous in their testimony. The way of Christ is far better. The broad way made big promises, but delivered little.

But there is a problem. Before one travels it, the broad way appears bright, exciting, and loaded with fulfillment. But the oasis of promised refreshment and satisfaction soon turns into a mirage. By way of contrast, before it is experienced, the way of Christ appears hard, restrictive, and austere. When it is experienced, however, it proves to be filled with joy, peace, and high adventure, as we are swept along in God's great plan for the ages.

A woman I know is living in sin with another woman's husband. She was looking for fulfillment and happiness in the experience, but she is miserable. As she sat and poured out the whole sordid mess, she wept bitter tears. The broad way leads to destruction. Her story could be repeated thousands of times.

A young man I know has tried the way of the world for years. Time after time the oasis turned to dust in his hands. The experience is consistent: hot, dry sand rather than the fulfillment he was seeking.

Jesus was right. Life does not consist in the abundance of possessions. The broad way is a subtle trap. It is easy to go that way, and the end thereof is the way of death. It leads to destruction.

Covetousness

I'm neither a hero nor a brave man. So, when I saw the sign I got a bit nervous. It was located between Jericho and the Dead Sea, a simple wooden sign that had the appearance of a normal everyday road sign you see anywhere in the world. But the message was different. The sign read: "Frontier Area—Proceeding Further Will Endanger Your Life." We were near the border of Jordan and Israel—no-man's-land. It was a beautiful, cloudless day, peaceful and serene. There was no indication of danger anywhere. There was only the shining sea, the soaring birds, and the warm breeze, but had we gone down that road we could have drawn some mortar, mchine gun, and sniper fire.

Life is like that. We need clear signs to tell us when we are nearing the frontier areas, to tell us when proceeding further would endanger our lives. And thank God, He has not left us to wander in the dark. The psalmist said, "Thy word is a lamp unto my feet, and a light unto my path" (Ps. 119:105). "There is a way which seemeth right unto a man, but the end thereof are the ways of death" (Prov. 14:12).

Take for instance, the path of pleasure. We are on a pleasure kick in the western world. Nothing is wrong with having fun, taking a vacation, relaxing in the sun, or enjoying sports. But, for the person who lives for pleasure, it soon takes more and more to satisfy. At first a weekend at Lake Okeboge is really neat. But that grows stale, so next time it's a trip to Miami Beach, then Hawaii. Then Pago Pago, then the Riviera, then a remote island off the coast of India. And pretty soon nothing is any fun any more. He's been everywhere, done everything, and it's all turned to dust. I've watched people take the path of pleasure and it's ruined their health and destroyed them; life has become a drag. Jesus said, "These things have I spoken unto you, that My joy might remain in you, and that your joy might be full" (John 15:11).

Accumulation of things is no better. And no wonder. Jesus said, "Take heed, and beware of covetousness, for a man's life consisteth not in the abundance of the things which he possesseth" (Luke 12:15). But some people have a hard time believing that statement. Laying up treasures on earth becomes a way of life. After they have stuffed their garage with two or three of the world's most exotic cars, and stuffed their home full of Persian rugs, original art, and expensive furniture, they fill their lawns with brass and alabaster bird baths. Jewels, furs, alligator shoes, and silks and satins fill their closets. Then they pick up a magazine and discover that to really be with it they need something else, because all they have has gone out of style.

The simple desire for financial security has led many a person into the money trap. You know the answer of the rich man who was asked how much money it took to bring happiness: "Just a little bit more." The Bible says, "He that loveth silver shall not be satisfied with silver; nor he that loveth abundance with increase; this is also vanity" (Ecc. 5:10). That's a promise. Silver and gold cannot satisfy. Certainly the Bible says you need food and raiment, but to wander into no-man's-land of the lust for pleasure and things and money endangers your life. And so God says, "Beware."

A Lesson from Ai

It was an overcast and cloudy day as we drove north from Jerusalem. In the distance there was a break in the clouds, and one hill was brightly illuminated under the brilliant Palestinian sun. Our guide said, "That's the city of Ai you see shining in the sun." My mind went back hundreds of years to another day when God taught His people an everlasting truth in that place.

The army of God had suffered a great defeat. Joshua was on

his face before the Lord crying out for an answer. What was wrong? He had received and believed God's promise: "There shall not any man be able to stand before thee all the days of thy life. As I was with Moses, so I will be with thee: I will not fail thee nor forsake thee" (Josh. 1:5). What had gone wrong? Had God failed in His word? "And the Lord said unto Joshua, 'Get thee up; wherefore liest thou thus upon thou face? Israel hath sinned, and they have also transgressed My covenant which I commanded them; for they have even taken of the accursed thing, and have also stolen, and dissembled also, and they have put it even among their own stuff' " (Josh. 7:10-11).

Simply stated, here's what had happened. God had told His people to consecrate all the treasure of the city of Jericho to Him. In response to God's command they put all the silver and gold, and vessels of brass and iron into the treasury of the house of the Lord. Well, almost all. A man named Achan had seen a few things he wanted for himself. He explained, "When I saw among the spoils a goodly Babylonish garment, and 20 shekels of silver, and a wedge of gold of 50 shekels weight, then I coveted them, and took them, and behold, they are hid in the earth in the midst of my own tent, and the silver under it" (Josh. 7:21). I saw, I coveted, and I took. What was his sin? Simple. He took for himself that which belonged to God.

Have you ever done that? Think about it for a minute. God has said, "My son, give Me thine heart" (Prov. 23:26). Who has your heart today? Does God have a part and something else or someone else the other? Are you offering God a splintered heart? The Bible says, "Set your affection on things above, not on things on the earth" (Col. 3:2). Why? Because the gods of this earth will fail you. They will prove false.

How do you spend your time? Serving the Lord or serving yourself? If you are your own god, your god is too small. The most mind-expanding thing you can do, the most exhilarating thing that will ever happen to your spirit, the most powerful thing you can do with your life is to learn how to devote your time to living for Jesus Christ. Don't try to keep it and use it for yourself. It belongs to Him. The Word of God gives us clear and positive direction on how to walk and talk with Him, how to lose our life and thereby find it.

Actually, when you reflect on the sin of Achan, it seems rather small in comparison with many sins the Bible speaks out against. Think again. To use for yourself that which rightly belongs to God is robbery. Years later, the Lord confronted His people with the same condemnation: "Will a man rob God? Yet ye have robbed me. But ye say, 'Wherein have we robbed Thee?' In tithes and offerings. Ye are cursed with a curse; for ye have robbed me, even this whole nation" (Mal. 3:8-9). All that we are and have rightly belong to Him. This day belongs to Him. It is the day that He made. Are we God's stewards and good stewards of God's property? "As every man hath received the gift, even so minister the same to another, as good stewards of the manifold grace of God" (1 Peter 4:10).

Develop a life-style that is right for you in light of your needs, your responsibilities, and the Word of God. If you have a family and use your home as a place to entertain guests and witness for Christ, you obviously need more dishes, a larger table, more chairs, and a bigger stove than a single girl in an apartment. If you use your car to haul kids to camp, you obviously need a larger automobile than a single guy in college. So think through on your situation and begin to make any adjustments that need to be brought in line with the life of discipleship. Proceeding further along an unscriptural path can endanger your life.

Pride

There is a sense in which pride is a good thing. Whenever my mother went to the grocery store she always combed her hair and put on a clean apron. There was something in her that wouldn't let her appear unkempt in public. Though she lived in poverty most of her life, she always tried to look her best. While some of the neighbors let their yards go to weeds, she always insisted that we keep the weeds down and the grass mowed. The house we lived in rented for $10 a month, and though it wasn't much of a place, we kept it painted and looking neat. We took a certain pride in our home and wanted it to look nice. Our family had a proper sense of dignity and worth. Today I see women in the supermarket wearing grubby cut-off jeans, 40 pounds overweight, with their hair in curlers, and I wish they would take a little pride in themselves like my mother did.

The Bible strongly warns about the hazards of pride: "When pride cometh, then cometh shame" (Prov. 11:2); "Everyone that is proud in heart is an abomination to the Lord" (16:5); "Pride goeth before destruction and an haughty spirit before a fall" (16:18). Paul warned that in the last days "men shall be lovers of their own selves, covetous, boasters, proud" (2 Tim. 3:2). This is the kind of pride that is an abomination to God. It is vain and foolish for a man who was made from the dust of the ground to be filled with arrogance and conceit. That kind of pride manifests itself in a disdain for others, an exaggerated opinion of one's ability or worth, a consuming desire for admiration and praise and a sickening display of boasting about one's accomplishments. That is what God hates. Not the man, but the pride that grips him. Why? Because pride is a weapon that the devil uses to keep men from God, thus to seal their eternal destruction.

We must remember our origins: created by God from the dust of the earth. "We have this treasure in earthen vessels, that the excellency of the power may be of God, and not of us" (2 Cor. 4:7).

Paul told the Corinthians: "For ye see your calling, brethren, how that not many wise men after the flesh, not many mighty, not many noble, are called; but God hath chosen the foolish things of the world to confound the wise; and God hath chosen the weak things of the world to confound the things which are mighty; and base things of the world, and things which are despised, hath God chosen, yea, and things which are not, to bring to nothing things that are, that no flesh should glory in His presence" (1 Cor. 1:26-29).

Prologue to Chapters 11 and 12

The life that is not grounded in the great doctrines of the Bible is lashed to a very shaky mooring. It is prone to be tossed to and fro by the false winds of man-made ideas. Deceivers abound and they lie in wait to fill our minds with falsehood.

As a new Christian, you will be confronted day by day with the ideas of atheists and agnostics, some of whom would take delight in trying to destroy your newly-found faith. Fortunately there are many fine books that can help you answer them. At first you may want to explore a few of the basic doctrines, so the next two chapters are designed for you.

Chapter 11 talks about some of the important doctrinal truths you should know. Most of them appear to be theoretical in nature, but they have practical implications. Chapter 12 talks about some of the practical day-by-day questions that arise about what the Bible says. Remember that your primary source of learning from God must always be His Word, so never allow another book to take its place in your life.

11

What the Bible Says—Doctrine

The Existence of God

To me, the greatest proof for the existence of God is answered prayer. Through the years I have received specific answers to prayer that demonstrated beyond question that when I pray there is a God in heaven who hears and answers. God has said, "Call unto Me, and I will answer thee, and show thee great and mighty things which thou knowest not" (Jer. 33:3).

My wife and I were in Pittsburgh in the early 1950s as faith missionaries to university students. Christmas rolled around and we had no money to buy gifts for our two kids, so we prayed. A couple of nights later Bill and Edie Newton from the First Presbyterian Church came up our walk carrying boxes. They told us the Lord had laid it on their hearts to do a little Christmas shopping for us. They brought in a beautiful red bike for our son, and a doll, doll clothes, ironing board, and toy iron for our daughter. We had not told anyone about our lack of funds. But the Lord had spoken to them and laid it on their hearts to help us out.

One thing I learned as a new Christian was this truth: "Be careful for nothing, but in everything, by prayer and supplication with thanksgiving, let your requests be known unto God. And the peace of God, which passeth all understanding, shall keep your hearts and minds through Christ Jesus" (Phil. 4:6-7). In everything. Nothing is too small or too large for God. He can handle it, and stands ready and willing to do so. Immediately? No, not always, but here again I've learned a lesson. His timing is perfect. He is never a minute late.

John Goodwin and I were on the campus of Penn State University in a meeting in one of the fraternity houses. The room was packed, and a fellow asked John how we knew there was a God. I wondered what John would say. His answer went something like this: First of all, there is a world-wide hunger to find God and to know Him in a personal way. Elaborate religious schemes have been devised from the remote primitive areas of the world to the highly sophisticated countries of the earth. Where does this universal hunger come from if not from God? Second, there is a general agreement around the world as to what is right and what is wrong. If there is no universal Lawgiver who has written His law in the hearts of men, how did it get there?

There is another way of looking at it. In our kitchen we have a remarkable stove. It can turn itself on, cook the food, and then turn itself off again! It can even clean its own oven! If you were to try to tell my children that the stove just happened, they would think you were nuts. Somebody made it. It's too perfect to have just fallen together by chance. It demands a creator and designer.

A noted space scientist concluded that for our universe to have just happened by chance is about as logical as believing that the Encyclopedia Britannica fell together as a result of an explosion in the print shop.

For me personally, there are some even greater reasons for believing in God. Each of us has the liberty to listen to someone and then decide for ourselves whether he is telling the truth or not. We can read a book and make the decision as to whether we believe the author or not. In my own mind I have chosen to believe the words of Jesus Christ, and I have concluded that the Lord had good reasons for doing what He did. Jesus prayed, "Father, the hour is come; glorify Thy Son that Thy Son also may glorify Thee" (John 17:1). Jesus believed in God and talked to Him in prayer. He said, "I have manifested Thy name unto the men which Thou gavest me out of the world" (17:6). Whose name? God's name, of course. He came to reveal God to man. He said, "He that hath seen Me hath seen the Father" (John 14:9). Who was He talking about? Joseph the carpenter? Hardly! He was talking about His Father in heaven. He taught His followers to pray and told them, "After this manner, therefore, pray ye: 'Our

Father, which art in heaven, Hallowed be thy name' " (Matt 6:9). Jesus taught that there is a God in heaven who listens to us when we pray.

People who don't believe in God fall into two categories. One is the *atheist,* who says there is no God. David, the man after God's own heart, wrote, "The fool hath said in his heart, 'There is no God' " (Ps. 14:1). The other is the *agnostic.* He is not sure. He doesn't know whether God exists or not.

The answer to honest agnosticism lies in the experiment of faith. And the agnostic owes it to himself to try it. If he knows that mixing chemical X with chemical Y always produces the same result, he has no reason to doubt its truth. He can try it for himself. There is a truth simply stated in the Bible that has proven true in millions of lives. "Therefore, if any man be in Christ, he is a new [creation]; old things are passed away; behold, all things are become new" (2 Cor. 5:17). The world is full of people who have taken that step of faith and can testify to its truth.

The Sovereignty of God

I hate the sound of sirens. A siren usually means trouble—someone is being rushed to the hospital; an accident has occurred; a building is on fire. Something unexpected has happened and people are on the way to handle the emergency. When you think of it, that's going to be one of the blessings of heaven: no panic buttons; no plan "B"; no sirens. Everything will be done according to the plan and will of God. God, who knows everything, is never taken by surprise.

"The Lord hath prepared His throne in the heavens, and His kingdom ruleth over all" (Ps. 103:19). The word *prepared* can be translated "fixed" or "established." From a study of other parts of Scripture we know the Lord's throne is one of glory, from which God, who made all, rules all. He prepared it and established it forever for Himself. He was not appointed to this position. He is the eternal God on His eternal throne, abiding by His eternal laws in His eternal kingdom. "For I know that the Lord is great, and that our Lord is above all gods. Whatsoever the Lord pleased, that did He in heaven, and in earth, in the seas, and all deep places" (Ps. 135:5-6). All the struggles of evil men or demons from hell cannot shake His sovereign rule.

What does this doctrine of the sovereignty of God mean to us?

How does this truth apply to our daily lives? Is it of practical value?

How many times have you heard people say, "I didn't understand it at the time, but now that I look back on it I can certainly see the hand of God in it all"? This was the case with Joseph when he was sold into slavery by his brothers. Years later, when they had come to Egypt to buy food, Joseph told them, "But as for you, ye thought evil against me; but God meant it unto good, to bring to pass, as it is this day, to save many people alive" (Gen. 50:20). God's hand was in it all.

As we contemplate today's world with its chaos and confusion, it is difficult at times to believe in the sovereignty of God. But Christian, take heart! If you are facing a difficulty today, remember that God rules over all. His sovereignty is universal. Other rulers, presidents, and kings come and go, but He is eternal. He is what He has been, He has been what He is, and He is what He shall be.

The Sufferings of Christ

Christians often ask why God allowed His Son to suffer and die for us. "Why couldn't He have found some other way?" they ask.

I thought about the sufferings Christ endured when I was visiting the Holy Land. It was really quite an experience to sit in the common hall of what had been the house of Pontius Pilate. Military men need pastimes to help while away the hours in the barracks, and Pilate's men found enjoyment in playing two or three games popular at the time. But they had the most fun when they were given prisoners to torment and ridicule. It was in that hall that Jesus provided them with a few hours of fun.

Our guide through Pilate's Hall was Sister Agnes of the Sisters of Zion. She was a small English lady with an amazing grasp of history, a sense of deep fulfillment in her work, and a love for the Lord Jesus that showed clearly in all she did.

She pointed us to the Scriptures that told of Jesus as He stood before Pilate, the Roman governor. When it became evident to the governor that the mob preferred Barabbas to Jesus, he scourged Jesus and delivered Him to the soldiers to be crucified. That was when the soldiers had their fun. "Then the soldiers of the governor took Jesus into the common hall, and gathered unto Him the whole band of soldiers. And they stripped Him, and put on Him a scarlet robe. And when they had platted a crown of thorns, they put it upon His head, and a reed in His right hand; and they bowed the knee before Him, and mocked Him saying, 'Hail, King of the Jews!' And they spit upon Him, and took the reed, and smote Him on the head. And after that they had mocked Him, they took the robe off from Him, and put His own raiment on Him, and led Him away to crucify Him" (Matt. 27:27-31).

Who knows how long the soldiers shoved Jesus around and beat Him before they stopped? One thing we do know is this: He permitted it to be done. At any time He could have called upon 12 legions of angels to come and wipe out the entire Roman band. The merciless scourging and the beating with the reed left Him battered and bloody. The prophet said, "His visage was so marred more than any man, and His form more than the sons of men" (Isa. 52:14). Why did Jesus permit it? Why did He let them lead Him away to be crucified? Read again the words of the prophet, "He is despised and rejected of men, a man of sorrows, and acquainted with grief; and we hid as it were our faces from Him; He was despised, and we esteemed Him not. Surely He hath borne our griefs, and carried our sorrows; yet we did esteem Him stricken, smitten of God, and afflicted. But he was wounded for our transgressions, He was bruised for our iniquities" (Isa. 53:3-6).

The sufferings of Jesus were for you and me. "But God commendeth His love toward us, in that, while we were yet sinners, Christ died for us" (Rom. 5:8).

The Importance of the Resurrection of Christ

Many scholars are convinced that a garden just outside the old city wall of Jerusalem is the place where Jesus Christ was buried after His crucifixion. It was discovered by General Gordon in 1883 and is now cared for by the Garden Tomb Association of England. It is a lovely place, in spite of the fact that just to the right there is a hill with the face of a skull on its rocky cliff. As I sat looking at it, I was reminded of the day that split the world's calendar and changed millions of lives.

Paul's capsule statement of the Gospel reads: "For I delivered unto you first of all that which I also received, how that Christ died for our sins according to the Scriptures; and that He was buried, and that He rose again the third day according to the Scriptures" (1 Cor. 15:3-4).

The fact of the resurrection has been the object of scorn and ridicule through the centuries. But Jesus plainly taught, "I am the resurrection, and the life. He that believeth in Me, though he were dead, yet shall he live. And whosoever liveth and believeth in Me shall never die" (John 11:25). Paul asked King Agrippa, "Why should it be thought a thing incredible with you, that God should raise the dead?" (Acts 26:8) The Apostle Paul knew the power of the resurrection of Christ. "But if the Spirit of Him that raised up Jesus from the dead dwell in you, He that raised up Christ from the dead shall also quicken your mortal bodies by His Spirit that dwelleth in you" (Rom. 8:11). Christian, take courage! The Holy Spirit of God who raised up Jesus from the dead lives in you! You have a power in your life that defies the limits of the mind of man. The Spirit of Him who raised up Jesus from the dead!

The Apostle Paul first met the risen Christ on the road to Damascus. He was out to put a stop to the spread of faith in this dead man. "As he journeyed he came near Damascus, and suddenly there shined round about him a light from heaven. And he fell to the earth, and heard a voice saying unto him, 'Saul, Saul, why persecutest thou Me?' And he said, 'Who art Thou, Lord?' And the Lord said, 'I am Jesus whom thou persecutest; it is hard for thee to kick against the pricks.' . . . And he was three days without sight, and neither did eat nor drink" (Acts 9:3-5, 9).

What was it that finally convinced this murderer of the followers of Jesus to become a Christian? The risen Christ. Paul said, "Of the Jews five times received I 40 stripes save one. Thrice was I beaten with rods, once was I stoned, thrice I suffered shipwreck, a night and a day I have been in the deep; in journeyings often, in perils of waters, in perils of robbers, in perils by mine own countrymen, in perils by the heathen, in perils in the city, in perils in the wilderness, in perils in the sea, in perils among false brethren, in weariness and painfulness, in watchings often, in hunger and thirst, in fastings often, in cold and nakedness" (2 Cor. 11:24-27).

What gave him the power to continue? What gave him the power to serve Christ? It was the risen Christ. "I can do all things through Christ which strengtheneth me" (Phil. 4:13).

Justification

A great question has boggled the minds of philosophers for hundreds of centuries: "How can sinful man stand before a holy and righteous God?" Man has looked at himself in his sinfulness and at God in His holiness and despaired of ever being able to stand before God. Even Job, an upright man who feared God, cried out, "If I wash myself with snow water, and make my hands never so clean, yet shalt Thou plunge me in the ditch, and mine own clothes shall abhor me. For He is not a man, as I am, that I should answer Him, and we should come together in judgment" (Job 9:30-32). Is there a way for sinners to be made righteous?

The Scriptures answer with a resounding *yes!* The Apostle Paul says, "Therefore being justified by faith, we have peace with God through our Lord Jesus Christ" (Rom. 5:1). In that passage the apostle uses the word *justified,* which is a legal term. It means the legal act of God by which He declares the sinner righteous, based on the perfect righteousness of Christ.

Let me illustrate. I recall standing in the front of the little church in my home town the night I was married. The wedding march was being played and all was in readiness for the ceremony. Had my best man whispered to me just as Virginia was starting down the long aisle, "What are you?" I would have answered, "Single." If he had asked the question as she approached the front of the church I would have again answered, "Single." Even after I had slipped the ring on her finger, the answer would have been the same.

Then came the awesome and dramatic moment when the minister said, "I now pronounce you man and wife." At that moment, in a split second, my legal standing was changed. I was now legally married. Had my best man asked the question again my answer would have been, "Married!" because the minister had declared it so. That is the point that the Apostle Paul makes in that great passage. Based on my relationship with the Lord Jesus Christ, I am now a partaker of His righteousness.

In another passage the Apostle Paul explains how it all came about. "He hath made Him to be sin for us, who knew no sin; that we might be made the righteousness of God in Him" (2 Cor. 5:21). Christ, who had no sin, was made sin that we who have no righteousness may be made righteous.

The Holy Spirit
In the United States weddings are generally conceded to be the

responsibility of the bride. It is her day, and she spends an enormous amount of time in preparation for the big event. Selecting the dress can take weeks. Deciding on the time and place, the color of the dresses for the bridesmaids, where the reception will be held, who will be invited, what refreshments will be served, and on and on. The bridegroom is there and plays an important role, but the day belongs to the bride.

In some places of the world the groom steals the show on the wedding day. All day he is feasted and praised. Then, after sunset, the people of the village line the street and he rides through the column of people on a magnificent white horse. The people light torches and hold them high in the air as the groom rides by so that his face might be illuminated and they might see him clearly. They themselves are hidden in the shadows. Their objective is to draw attention to the bridegroom.

As we read the New Testament it becomes clear to us that the Holy Spirit is content to remain in the shadows as He points men and women to the person of Jesus Christ. He has no desire to call attention to Himself. "He shall testify of Me," Jesus said (see John 15:26).

Although this is true, it is important that we study the Person and work of the Spirit of God. First of all, He is a person. Jesus said, "And I will pray the Father, and He shall give you another Comforter, that He may abide with you forever, even the Spirit of truth, whom the world cannot receive, because it seeth Him not, neither knoweth Him. But ye know Him, for He dwelleth with you, and shall be in you" (John 14:16-17). He is not just a figurative expression of divine energy. He is a Person. He is one of the Members of the Trinity, and as such He is God. When Peter rebuked Ananias for his lies against the Holy Spirit, he reminded him that he had not "lied unto men, but unto God" (Acts 5:4). The Holy Spirit was sent on His ministry by both the Father and the Son. "But the Comforter, which is the Holy Ghost, whom the Father will send in My name, He shall teach you all things, and bring all things to your remembrance, whatsoever I have said unto you" (John 14:26).

The Apostle Paul gave two warnings regarding the ministry of the Holy Spirit in our lives. The first is, "Grieve not the Holy Spirit of God, whereby ye are sealed unto the day of redemption" (Eph. 4:30). We grieve the Holy Spirit by living contrary to the

Word of God in a life of disobedience to the Lord. It is God's desire that we live holy and pure lives; and when we permit known sin to remain unconfessed, the Spirit of God is grieved.

Paul's second warning is, "Quench not the Spirit" (1 Thes. 5:19). We quench the Spirit by not following His guidance in some service that the Lord would have us undertake. We must be sensitive to His leading and follow Him in instant obedience.

Volumes could be written on the Person and work of the Holy Spirit, but something to keep in mind is that He guides us according to the Word of God, never contrary to it. The desire of the Spirit is that we submit to His control and guidance. It is possible to understand much about Him and at the same time be living according to our own desires. His desire is to glorify Jesus Christ in and through us.

The Second Coming of Christ

We were in Christchurch, New Zealand participating in an evangelistic thrust during the Tenth Annual British Commonwealth Games. Scores of churches had banded together to provide an outreach for the Gospel to the hundreds of overseas visitors. The highlight of the games was that the Queen of England was to present the medals to the winners. She was flying in, and my wife and I had joined the thousands of others to see her arrival as she and some of the rest of the Royal Family came from Great Britain. Every eye was straining to catch the first glimpse of the huge silver plane as it appeared in the sky. A mood of joy and expectation ran through the crowd as the time drew near.

The police were walking back and forth in the street trying to keep people behind the ropes they had stretched along the curb. The crowd was excited, noisy, and everyone was jostling and shoving in an effort to be in the best possible place. The sun was beating down, hardly any breeze was in the air, and the people who had been standing there for two and three hours were showing the signs of getting a rather severe sunburn. But no one seemed to mind the heat or the crowds or the fact that his feet hurt from standing on the concrete sidewalk. The excitement of the event itself completely overshadowed all the discomforts of the situation.

Then someone shouted, "I see it! There it is." And, sure enough, high in the sky, many miles distant you could see the tiny speck of silver glinting in the sun. It drew nearer, made its approach, and landed. The queen and her party stepped out, and made their way to the podium where she made a brief speech to the crowd. Then they got into their limousine and slowly drove by those of us lined up against the ropes. They smiled and waved and we smiled and waved back. In a moment, it was all over. But the exciting memory remains.

A verse of Scripture says, "Teaching us that, denying ungodliness and worldly lusts, we should live soberly, righteously, and godly in this present world, looking for that blessed hope, and the glorious appearing of the great God and our Saviour Jesus Christ" (Titus 2:12-13). In the same way that the people of New Zealand looked for the arrival of their queen, so we should be looking for the coming of our King. It's a blessed hope, a happy hope, and a sure hope, because Jesus Himself said, "I will come again" (John 14:3). What a difference it would make in our daily lives if we lived life on tiptoe, expectantly, with a sense of excitement permeating our spirits, looking for that glorious coming of Christ, "who gave Himself for us, that He might redeem us from all iniquity, and purify unto Himself a peculiar people, zealous of good works" (Titus 2:14).

For many Christians a doctrine such as the second coming of Christ is often questioned—not the truth of the doctrine, which is abundantly clear in the Scriptures, but the practical value of the teaching is sometimes hard for them to understand. Is the Second Coming merely a teaching given to scare sinners into the kingdom or something to provide fuel for the fires of disagreement among theologians?

First, let's look at the question of Christians using this teaching as a spiritual bogeyman to scare people into the kingdom of God. God has, in fact, used fear as a motivation. "By faith Noah, being warned of God of things not seen as yet, moved with fear, prepared an ark to the saving of his house; by the which he condemned the world, and became heir of the righteousness which is by faith" (Heb. 11:7). And it is true that many people have repented of their sins and turned to Christ under the teaching of the Lord's return.

As you read the Scriptures, you see that this doctrine is meant to be a source of comfort to the believers. It permeates Paul's first letter to the Thessalonians. And he does not say, "Scare one another to death with these words." He says, "For the Lord Himself shall descend from heaven with a shout, with the voice of the archangel, and with the trump of God, and the dead in Christ shall rise first. Then we which are alive and remain shall be caught up together with them in the clouds, to meet the Lord in the air, and so shall we ever be with the Lord. Wherefore comfort one another with these words" (1 Thes. 4:16-18). It is a comfort to know that one day all the wrongs will be made right, the inhumanity and injustice of this world will be brought to a halt, and truth, goodness, and righteousness will win out.

This brings us to our second point. The second coming of Christ puts history in its proper framework. History is not cyclical, going around and around, repeating itself with no stopping place. History is linear, on a straight line, heading for a grand climax; there *is* a stopping place. Paul says, "For God has allowed us to know the secret of His plan, and it is this: He purposes in His sovereign will that all human history shall be consummated in Christ, that everything that exists in heaven or earth shall find its perfection and fulfillment in Him" (Eph. 1:9-10, PH).

The third practical outcome of this doctrine is stated by the Apostle John: "Beloved, now are we the sons of God, and it doth not yet appear what we shall be. But we know that, when He shall appear, we shall be like Him; for we shall see Him as He is. And every man that hath this hope in him purifieth himself, even as He is pure" (1 John 3:2-3).

The desire of every Christian is to meet the Lord while living a life of loving obedience to Him. The Scriptures are clear. No one knows his appointed time to be ushered into the presence of Christ, whether through the natural end of his life or the glorious appearing of the Great God and our Saviour Jesus Christ. Day by day we are prompted to a life of fellowship and communion with Him.

Almost every mention of the Second Coming given in Scripture is in the context of a warning to be prepared. Like weather bulletins before a storm, these warnings are for us so we may be prepared.

After obedient Chicagoans had removed their snow tires by April 1, 1975, the worst snow in eight years hit the city. Almost a foot of snow fell in some parts of town. Had people known what was going to happen, they would never have taken off the snow tires. But, of course, there was no way of knowing what was going to happen. The law was plain—all snow tires must be removed by April 1. The results were disastrous.

It took me five hours to drive from Wheaton to O'Hare Airport—a trip that usually takes a little more than 30 minutes. Hundreds of cars were stalled in snow drifts. Other hundreds ran out of gas and had to be abandoned. Here was a city with a foot of snow, with hundreds of abandoned cars and trucks, and with the passable roads glutted with thousands of slow-moving vehicles. Snow tires would have kept most of them moving, but the snow tires were safely stored away for another year. If people could only have known.

There is an alarming parallel to this story in the spiritual realm. I'm sure most people realize that one day they are going to stand before God. Somewhere, in one way or another, someone must have told them. Popular songs talk about that great judgment that's coming. Radio and television pastors and evangelists share the message constantly. "Prepare to meet thy God." I'm sure people *know* it, but they ignore the message. I was in Washington, D.C. talking with a man who works in a Satellite Weather Warning Commission. He told me that Darwin, Australia had received repeated warnings regarding the cyclone that devastated their city. Many lives could have been saved had they heeded the warnings that had been given.

A day is coming when all of us will bow before the Lord Jesus Christ. "That at the name of Jesus every knee should bow, of things in heaven, and things in earth, and things under the earth; and that every tongue should confess that Jesus Christ is Lord, to the glory of God the Father" (Phil. 2:10-11). People will have nothing to hide behind. But it is possible to make peace with God. The Apostle Paul said, "Therefore being justified by faith, we have peace with God through our Lord Jesus Christ" (Rom. 5:1).

12

Making Doctrine Practical

I recall the first new car I ever owned. It was a 1956 Dodge, with beautiful fins that swept up in back, push-button drive, and three colors of paint. I picked it up in Detroit the day that model came out. I drove from Detroit to Pittsburgh and arrived at three in the morning. I got the family out of bed and we took a ride around the block. We were so excited we could hardly sleep. It was hard to believe that this big, beautiful automobile was really ours.

The next morning I went out to the garage and inspected it again. In the glove compartment I found the owner's manual which told me all about the car: how much oil it took, how often to change the oil and oil filter, how much air to keep in the tires and how often to rotate them.

I could have had one of two reactions. I could have thought to myself, *Who do they think they are, telling me what to do with my car. I bought it, paid for it, it's mine. I'll do as I please.* Or I could have thought, *Isn't that great! Here's all this good information.* My reaction was the latter, because I realized that the company which had built the car had written the manual. If anyone should know what's best for the car it should be the people who made it. And their purpose in giving me the manual was not to bind me or restrict me but to enable me to get the most trouble-free miles out of the car. I gladly submitted myself to the authority of the manual. It is the same with life: we listen to the Creator or we can ignore Him if we choose.

The Bible

God made life and gave it to you and me to enjoy. Along with life He gave us a manual that tells how it is to be lived—the Holy Bible. He has not given us the Bible to bind or restrict us, but to help us get the most trouble-free years out of life.

Some days ago I was thinking about our bicentennial and the history of our country. As I reflected on the Constitution of the United States I was challenged again with what a remarkable document it is. It was written by dedicated and brilliant men. It is a treasure we all hold dear. But what do you find at the end? Amendments!

Contrast that with the Bible. God has given us the law of the world. Do you find any amendments at the end? No, quite to the contrary. We are told, "For I testify unto every man that heareth the words of the prophecy of this book. If any man shall add unto these things, God shall add unto him the plagues that are written in this book. And if any man shall take away from the words of the book of this prophecy, God shall take away his part out of the book of life, and out of the holy city, and from the things which are written in this book" (Rev. 22:18-19).

In addition to being authoritative and inspired, the Bible is also indispensable. It is indispensable for my growth and guidance. Without it I have no God-given goals and no guidelines for godly living. I am adrift at sea without compass or rudder. I am lost in the wilderness without map and guide. Without the Bible I find no food for my soul and no lamp for my feet. It is indispensable.

A widespread idea exists that the Bible is not true. Many professors at our major universities go out of their way to destroy a student's faith in the Scriptures. But, such faith-destroying ideas are not found only on campus. Even in some churches you hear the same thing. I heard one preacher who said that the blood of Christ was of no more value than the blood of a cat!

One of the first things that attracted me to the Bible was the lives of some people who were living by its teachings. I would visit their homes and find a warmth and love that prevailed. Through the years I have observed that the people who try to pattern their lives after the message of the Scriptures are good, hard-working, honest folk.

Another reason for believing the Bible is the teaching of

Christ Himself on the subject. In His prayer to His heavenly Father, He prayed for His followers and said, "Sanctify them through Thy truth. Thy Word is truth" (John 17:17).

Jesus Himself believed the Scriptures. After His resurrection from the dead, Jesus did not object to His followers' unbelief of the angels at the tomb, or to their slowness of heart to believe the women. He objected to their slowness of heart to believe the Bible. Luke tells us, "Then He said unto them, 'O fools, and slow of heart to believe all that the prophets have spoken'" (Luke 24:25).

I was talking to a college student one day who said he didn't believe the Bible was all that great. So I asked him what he would do if a publishing company offered him a million dollars to write a book. There would be only one stipulation on the part of the publisher. The author had to guarantee that after his book was published, men and women from every walk of life would be eager to take his book to every tongue and tribe and translate it into the language of the people just so the people could learn its message. Would be undertake the writing of this book? He laughed and said that he didn't think he could write such a book.

Of course not. There's only one book on earth like that—the Holy Bible. But the issue is not only whether or not we *believe* the Bible, but are we *living* by its teachings?

God's Revelation to Man
How to make contact with God is a mystery to most people. Though they can comprehend clearly the power of God or the greatness and majesty of God or the glory of God, they are totally in the dark as to how to approach Him in a vital and living experience. The man paddling down the Amazon in his dugout canoe hunting jaguar is just as much in the dark as the American college student driving around on campus in his Jaguar. The good news that God has revealed Himself in His Word is foreign to both of them.

Only the Gospel reveals how a man can communicate with God and how he can know that God is pleased with him, has forgiven his sins, has taken him into His family, and has given him the assurance of heaven.

I could take you today to a lovely temple in the Far East and introduce you to a beautiful young girl who serves there. You would be struck with her beauty, charm, and poise. But you'd notice something strange: her index finger on her right hand is missing. When you ask her about it, she would tell you she burned it off. If you ask her why, she will tell you it was an effort on her part to make contact with God and somehow receive the assurance from Him of the forgiveness of her sins.

I could also take you to a village where once a year the people perform a strange ceremony. From dawn till dusk they slash and beat themselves with whips and cut themselves with knives. Then at dusk they take the one whom they consider most worthy and crucify him. If you ask them why they do all this, they will tell you they are trying to atone for their sins.

That is the reality of religions around the world. Witchcraft, religious teachings from India, devil worship, drugs—the list is staggering. Man-made, Satan-inspired schemes. Thank God for the simple Gospel—the fact that God is not playing peekaboo with us through the clouds, but has taken the initiative, reached down to us in grace and mercy, and revealed Himself clearly and distinctly in the person of Jesus Christ.

The Lord's Day and Church

First impressions are lasting inpressions. The first time I heard Dawson Trotman speak he shared two verses that I've never forgotten. He had just told a dramatic story to point out the important truth that it matters how you spend your time on the Lord's Day. It does affect your usefulness to God.

The Scripture he shared was Isaiah 58:13-14: "If thou turn away thy foot from the Sabbath, from doing thy pleasure on My holy day, and call the Sabbath a delight, the holy of the Lord, honorable; and shalt honor Him, not doing thine own ways, nor finding thine own pleasure, nor speaking thine own words; then shalt thou delight thyself in the Lord; and I will cause thee to ride upon the high places of the earth, and feed thee with the heritage of Jacob thy father. For the mouth of the Lord hath spoken it."

It is true that Jesus taught that "the Sabbath was made for man, and not man for the Sabbath; therefore the Son of man is Lord also of the Sabbath" (Mark 2:27-28). But does that mean we are to treat the Lord's Day in the same way as the non-

Christian, buying and selling and leaving God out of the picture? Hardly. This day should be set aside as a day of rest for our bodies and refreshment for our souls. The passage from Isaiah spoke of this day as a delight. Too often young men and women have turned from keeping the Lord's Day because it was made distasteful and burdensome. Nothing could have been further from the mind of God when He provided us with this special day.

Jesus healed people on the Sabbath, which infuriated the religious leaders of His day. They condemned Him and accused Him of acting in an irreligious manner. On two occasions He asked them about how they treated their domestic animals. Did they feed them? If one of them fell in a ditch would they help it get out? The record tells us that His accusers were put to silence. It is perfectly fitting and proper to do works of mercy and necessity on the Lord's Day.

The Old Testament speaks of the Sabbath as being set aside to remember the mighty act of God in creation. "Wherefore the children of Israel shall keep the Sabbath, to observe the Sabbath throughout their generations, for a perpetual covenant. It is a sign between Me and the children of Israel for ever; for in six days the Lord made heaven and earth, and on the seventh day He rested, and was refreshed" (Exodus 31:16-17).

In the New Testament a new and powerful act of God is commemorated by the Lord's Day: the resurrection of the Lord Jesus Christ. Once every seven days, on the first day of the week, Christians gather in worship to remember the Lord's Day, the day He rose in victory over death. It, therefore, should be a day of celebration, a day of praise, joy, and thanksgiving.

The family picnic was always the big event of the year. All the aunts, uncles, cousins, brothers, and sisters would gather for a huge picnic. The ladies would out-do themselves in providing cakes, pies, fried chicken, and potato salad. We would play tag and baseball, eat watermelon, and have a great time. It was exciting to get together with the family.

I think that's why I love to go to church. We gather in the Father's house with our brothers and sisters in Christ for wonderful fellowship and inspiration. David felt the same way. "One thing have I desired of the Lord, that will I seek after: that I may dwell in the house of the Lord all the days of my life, to behold the beauty of the Lord, and to inquire in His temple"

(Ps. 27:4). He experienced the same joy in gathering together with the people of God. "I was glad when they said unto me, 'Let us go into the house of the Lord' " (Ps. 122:1).

Some think the church should be a perfect place for perfect people. But the church never was intended to be a gathering place for super-saints, but a repair shop for people who are having problems.

Others ask why there are so many different types of churches with varying forms in their order and worship. You will find services that are somber, happy, majestic, quiet, and enthusiastic. Something for everybody. The church that would put one person to sleep inspires another to glorious heights of worship and reverence. God has looked upon His worshipers, who vary in a thousand ways in their likes and dislikes, and in His grace has provided styles of worship to fit each of them.

Another reason why I enjoy going to church is that the church is the great leveller. David said, "I am a companion of all them who fear Thee, and of those who keep Thy precepts" (Ps. 119:63). David, the king, found companionship and fellowship with the people of God. Solomon, his son, testified to the same truth, "The rich and poor meet together; the Lord is the maker of them all" (Prov. 22:2). When I pray in church, I come to the throne of grace with the man who owns the bank and the man who keeps the bank clean. God is no respecter of persons and in the pew we are all one in Christ.

You and Miracles

A person's belief about miracles will, for one thing, depend upon his views of the universe. If he believes that the laws of nature are self-existent and set in operation by chance, then of course, they cannot change or be changed. But if we think of them as having been designed by God, then we must admit the possibility of their being altered on some special occasion.

We all know people who act in a certain manner, but on special occasions have a radical change of behavior. I know a college professor who is a very sedate, quiet, dignified man. He never changes. Well, almost never. You should see him with his little granddaughter. He rolls on the floor with her, sings, and makes funny faces to hear her laugh. His usual behavior is altered on those special occasions.

We cannot deny the fact that God could do something quite different with His universal laws if a situation arose that required it. He found it necessary to part the Red Sea, to send the ravens to feed His discouraged prophet, to inspire faith in the heart of His timid servant by causing a fleece to be damp with dew while all around it was dry. That's the heart of the matter concerning the miracles of Jesus. If He is God, He could perform miracles.

The first miracle of Jesus, when He turned water into wine, is recorded in the second chapter of John. Now what's so strange about water being changed to a form of grape juice? It's done every year all over the world. The rain falls from the sky, the vine drinks it in through the roots and when the grapes appear in clusters, they contain grape juice. If Jesus Christ, the Lord of the universe, wanted to speed up the process for this special occasion, He could do it, and He did.

When John the Baptist needed a word of encouragement while he languished in prison, Jesus reminded him of His miracles to bolster his faith. "Now, when John had heard in the prison the works of Christ, he sent two of his disciples, and said unto Him, 'Art thou He that should come, or do we look for another?' Jesus answered and said unto them, 'Go and show John again those things which ye do hear and see: the blind receive their sight, and the lame walk, the lepers are cleansed, and the deaf hear, the dead are raised up, and the poor have the gospel preached to them' " (Matt. 11:2-5).

When Jesus found it necessary to do something out of the ordinary, His disciples found it surprising and hard to comprehend. On one such occasion they were in the midst of a lake and were in danger of drowning. "And He arose, and rebuked the wind, and said unto the sea, 'Peace, be still.' And the wind ceased, and there was a great calm. And He said unto them, 'Why are ye so fearful? How is it that ye have no faith?' And they feared exceedingly, and said one to another, 'What manner of Man is this, that even the wind and the sea obey Him?' " (Mark 4:39-41)

Obviously the question about the miracles of Jesus is not, 'Are miracles possible?" but "Who is He?" The Bible teaches that He is the God-Man. "Without controversy great is the mystery of godliness: God was manifest in the flesh, justified in the Spirit, seen of angels, preached unto the Gentiles, believed on in the world, received up into glory" (1 Tim. 3:16). As such, all things are possible to Him, even miracles.

Total Depravity—What It Means

Certain foods must be wrapped in waxed paper or put in plastic bags before you put them in the refrigerator. If you don't, the odor from these foods will permeate everything else.

In one sense, that's what the doctrine of the total depravity of man is all about. This doctrine does not teach that every man is as bad as he can get. On the contrary, we've all read of accounts of men bravely risking their lives to save people who were unknown to them. During World War II, I had been wounded. In the face of withering machine gun and mortar fire two men grabbed me and risked their lives getting me to an aid station. Men and women all over the world who profess no relationship with God perform kind, loving, and humanitarian acts of mercy.

Nevertheless, the doctrine of total depravity is true. The Bible teaches that every area of life has been effected by sin. "This I say, therefore, and testify in the Lord, that ye henceforth walk not as other Gentiles walk, in the vanity of their mind, having the understanding darkened, being alienated from the life of God through the ignorance that is in them, because of the blindness of their heart; who, being past feeling, have given themselves over unto lasciviousness, to work all uncleanness with greediness" (Eph. 4:17-19).

Depravity, according to Jesus, has its root in the heart. "For from within, out of the heart of men, proceed evil thoughts, adulteries, fornications, murders, thefts, covetousness, wickedness, deceit, lasciviousness, an evil eye, blasphemy, pride, foolishness. All these evil things come from within, and defile the man" (Mark 7:21-23).

The Bible's solution to man's depravity is found in the redemptive work of Christ. "But ye have not so learned Christ. If so be that ye have heard Him, and have been taught by Him, as the truth is in Jesus: That ye put off concerning the former manner of life the old man, which is corrupt according to the deceitful lusts, and be renewed in the spirit of your mind; and that ye put on the new man, which after God is created in righteousness and true holiness" (Eph. 4:20-24).

Original Sin and Sinners

He was really struggling, but try as he might, he just could not understand the idea of original sin. He was a graduate of the United States Air Force Academy, and a brilliant young man. I had showed him passage after passage from the Bible but the basic truth of how Adam's sin affected all of us still escaped him. Then I told him a story that cleared it up for him.

It seems there was a flight commander who took off from the airfield one day with his group. He had his orders and his flight plans. Everything seemed normal and routine as they flew over the ocean. Then he decided to leave the course he had been ordered to take and launch out on a path of his own choosing. Disaster struck. One by one the planes ran out of fuel and plunged into the dark waters. They were lost.

With that as a background, we looked again at Romans 5:12: "Wherefore, as by one man sin entered into the world, and death by sin, and so death passed upon all men, for all have sinned." Adam had led us on a course that plunged us all in the murky depth of sin. "For all have sinned, and come short of the glory of God" (Rom. 3:23). We sin because we are sinners, following Adam's pattern.

God's plan of redemption was costly. The cross of Christ not only shows us the love of God, but the awfulness of sin. Jesus Christ willingly took our sins and paid the penalty of death. "For as by one man's disobedience many were made sinners, so by the obedience of One shall many be made righteous" (Rom. 5:19). God laid on Him the iniquity of us all. Surely He hath borne our sins and carried our sorrows. And not only has God imputed the sin of man to Christ, but there is one final step. You and I receive life, eternal life, through Jesus Christ. "For by grace are ye saved through faith; and that not of yourselves, it is the gift of God; not of works, lest any man should boast" (Eph. 2:8-9).

Satan

Early each morning I place myself under the Lordship and protection of Jesus Christ. If I choose His Lordship I will choose against myself and thus be kept from the foolish and hurtful lusts that war against the soul. I want to be under His protection because I have it on good authority that our adversary, the devil, as a roaring lion is walking around seeking whom he may devour (see 1 Peter 5:8).

If you are under the protection of Jesus, you are in a place of authority and power. The Bible teaches us that "greater is He that is in you than he that is in the world" (1 John 4:4). Therefore in the name of Jesus Christ you can resist the devil and he will flee from you.

In the Bible the devil is called the evil one. Moral evil is his basic and dominant attribute. According to the Bible, Satan is fundamentally a liar and his kingdom is founded on lies and deceit. His power lies primarily in his ability to trick you into thinking that what he proposes is good. The devil tricked Eve into thinking that to disobey God was good, that in doing so she would be like God. When you are tempted by the devil he will try to deceive you with the lie that good can be gotten at the cost of doing wrong.

One of his chief purposes on earth is to keep non-Christians from a saving experience with Christ. Paul says, "If our Gospel be hid it is hid to them that are lost, in whom the god of this world hath blinded the minds of them which believe not, lest the light of the glorious Gospel of Christ, who is the image of God, should shine unto them" (2 Cor. 4:3-4). Therefore when you pray for friends and relatives who are outside of Christ, you should pray that the Spirit of God will remove the blindfold that Satan has put over their eyes, and that they might see the light of Christ.

Another of Satan's objectives is to discredit the Word of God. He often uses false teachers who appear to represent God. They were active in Paul's day. "For such are false apostles, deceitful workers, transforming themselves into the apostles of Christ. And no marvel, for Satan himself is transformed into an angel of light. Therefore, it is no great thing if his ministers also be transformed as the ministers of righteousness, whose end shall be according to their works" (2 Cor. 11:13-15). Sometimes he will use some "scholar," who will appear intelligent and honorable and will in a skillful manner lead people to think that they can't believe the Bible.

This is all part of the enemy's strategy to deceive. He hates and fears the Word of God. He cannot cope with the sword of the Holy Spirit.

Satan is a defeated foe and he knows it. He was defeated at the cross where Jesus Christ "having spoiled principalities and powers, He made a show of them openly, triumphing over them in it" (Col. 2:15). You can take your stand as a Christian in the victory of Jesus Christ. The devil and all the principalities and powers, and demons of hell were conquered by our crucified and risen Saviour.

The first promise in the Bible concerning the warfare between Christ and Satan was fulfilled at the cross as Jesus dealt the deciding blow to the devil. He spoiled him, conquered him, disabled him, and made a show of him openly. Never had the devil and all his hosts received such a devastating defeat. Ultimately he will meet his final doom. "And the devil that deceived them was cast into the lake of fire and brimstone, where the beast and the false prophet are, and shall be tormented day and night forever and ever" (Rev. 20:10).

The Occult

The First World Congress on Sorcery in Bogota, Colombia attracted 5,000 people and over 1,000 foreign delegates in August, 1975. Sessions were held on astrology, sorcery, divination, parapsychology, and alchemy. Voodoo and other occult rituals were performed by practitioners from Africa, Brazil, Haiti, and Colombia. Occult communication via palmistry and astrology were attempted. Many kept up a vigil, hoping to see Beelzebub appear in person.

Parker Brothers reports that in the United States Ouija boards are outselling the game of Monopoly. Spiritualists say the messages of these boards come from "guides" or "angels." People who involve themselves in it say some unseen, intelligent force seems to control them and relay these messages. Occult literature is everywhere. This morning I was in the supermarket in our neighborhood and looked at the small booklets for sale at the checkout stand. Among those for sale were some on witchcraft, omens, foretelling the future, astrology, Satan, and palmistry.

The Bible has many things to say about this. Early in the record of divine revelation God warned His people, "When thou art come into the land which the Lord thy God giveth thee, thou shalt not learn to do after the abominations of those nations. There shall not be found among you anyone that maketh his son or his daughter pass through the fire, or that useth divination, or an observer of times, or an enchanter, or a witch, or a charmer, or a consultor of familiar spirits, or a wizard, or a necromancer. For all that do these things are an abomination unto the Lord; and because of these abominations the Lord thy God doth drive them out from before thee" (Deut. 18:9-12).

The first of these mentioned had to do with causing children to pass through the fire. This was a ritual to the Phoenician god Molech. Idolatry was popular because it appealed to people's lower natures and the idol could be seen. For years these people ignored the warnings of God.

The second is a warning against divination, the practice of foretelling future events or discovering hidden knowledge. This consisted of everything from the simple practice of drawing lots or consulting with images to the complicated practice of slaying animals and examining the liver (Ezek. 21:21).

There follows a remarkable list of people who were in touch with the demon world and who possessed remarkable powers because they were in the possession of the devil. They conversed with demons and consulted with magic charms. The Lord gave clear warnings to His people to avoid all such people and practices.

These examples of the occult have their roots in ancient, demon-inspired paganism. God's judgment on ancient Babylon was sure. "Thou art wearied in the multitude of thy counsels. Let now the astrologers, the stargazers, the monthly prognosticators, stand up, and save thee from these things that shall come upon thee. Behold, they shall be like stubble; and the fire shall burn them; they shall not deliver themselves from the power of the flame; there shall not be a coal to warm at, nor fire to sit before it" (Isa. 47:13-14). These pagan sorcerers and magicians were the devil's counterpart to the prophets of God. They were feared and held in high esteem and often called upon to reveal the future and explain difficult problems. Some would repeat secret words that had special meanings in their demon-inspired rituals.

For centuries Satan confined his occult practices pretty much to the remote areas of the world, but in recent years he has become more open in his activities in America as our nation drifts farther and farther from God. There has been a remarkable rise in the use of drugs, which have always been a part of satanic ritual and worship. It is one of the signs of the last times. "Now the Spirit speaketh expressly that, in the latter times, some shall depart from the faith, giving heed to seducing spirits, and doctrines of devils" (1 Tim. 4:1).

False Doctrine

The devil's lies sometimes appear more loving, warm, generous, and gracious than the truth of God. Satan can make the most abominable heresy look pleasing and appealing to the eye. When he led Eve astray in the garden, he told her that there was really no harm in what he suggested. In fact he told her there were great spiritual advantages to following his advice.

Most false doctrine is like that. It never suggests that there is only one way to heaven. The teachers of false doctrine are generally broadminded at this point. "There are many ways to God," they will tell you. "God is not so narrow and restrictive as to provide only one way!" Now doesn't that sound more generous and reasonable than to believe that Jesus is the only way? No, not really. When you study the matter you can see the beautiful truth of God's way of salvation. But to the new Christian or to the uninstructed, false doctrine can be appealing.

Take the matter of the Bible. The false teachers will say, "Oh sure, the Bible is a religious book. But there are many religious books in the world and we can learn from all of them. Why limit yourself to just the one? And beside that, hasn't it been proven that the Bible is full of myths and errors?" It is true that the world is full of religious books and many of them contain much that is helpful. But there is one difference. The Bible is the Word of God to man. All others are the writings of men who try to explain to us their views of God and the holy life. Often you will hear a person teaching the false doctrine that the Bible merely contains the Word of God. This would lead us to conclude that it also contains the word of man.

Remember that the Bible does not merely contain the Word of God. It *is* the Word of God. "No prophecy of the Scripture is of any private interpretation. For the prophecy came not in old time by the will of man, but holy men of God spoke as they were moved by the Holy Ghost" (2 Peter 1:20-21).

Consider the false doctrine that is running rampant in the

world concerning the person of Jesus Christ. "Naturally we all agree that he was a good man," they say. "And we agree that he was a great teacher, but there have been many great men and fine teachers in the world." Then they begin to equate Jesus with other religious leaders. They tell you to study them all and learn from them.

However, Nicodemus was right when he concluded that Jesus was a teacher come from God. Jesus said, "For I came down from heaven, not to do Mine own will, but the will of Him that sent Me" (John 6:38). We take our stand with the Apostle Peter. "Lord, to whom shall we go? Thou hast the words of eternal life. And we believe and are sure that Thou art that Christ, the Son of the living God" (6:68-69).

The more truth a false doctrine contains, the more deadly it is. When a new one appears that is blatantly spurious we can spot it immediately. But many an unwary soul has been led astray by a false doctrine that sounded good and appeared to have the teachings of the Bible as its source.

One good rule of thumb is to watch out for those people who claim to have found a new truth or discovered new light that had been hidden for centuries but now is revealed. This is to suggest that the apostles were in the dark on the matter, and a new revelation has been given. Christian, remember where your faith is founded. You "are built upon the foundation of the apostles and prophets, Jesus Christ Himself being the chief cornerstone" (Eph. 2:20).

Today thousands of people are led astray into false cults, strange doctrines, Eastern religions, and the occult. This shouldn't surprise us, for Paul's advice to Timothy is good for us today. "But evil men and seducers shall become worse and worse, deceiving, and being deceived. But continue thou in the things which thou hast learned and hast been assured of, knowing of whom thou hast learned them, and that from a child thou hast known the holy scriptures, which are able to make thee wise unto salvation through faith which is in Christ Jesus" (2 Tim. 3:13-15).